Visible Strengths,
Hidden Scars

Visible Strengths, Hidden Scars

Shegitu Kebede

This book is a work of non-fiction. All stories and accounts are true.

Copyright © 2011 by Shegitu Kebede

All rights reserved, including the right to reproduce this book or portions thereof in any form whatsoever.

ISBN: 978-0-615-99295-2

2nd Edition

Book cover and layout designed by:

Monster of the Midwest, LLC.
1300 Nicollet Ave.
Suite 3101
Minneapolis, MN 55403
(612) 886 - 2197

Photo courtesy of Mark Luinenburg

Manufactured in the United States of America by Gleason Printing, Inc.

Foreword

    I got to know Shegitu on an airplane flight from Minneapolis to New Orleans in 2002. Shegitu and I were sitting side by side, flying to a national conference focused on children, youth, and families. On that day, I was feeling particularly sad and Shegitu sensed it. She asked me some gentle questions initiating our conversation and then offered comforting support. I will always keep a sweet memory of how Shegitu helped me that day with her selfless way of being. Throughout the flight our conversation became intertwined with stories about ourselves. There I learned about her arduous life in Ethiopia and the Kenyan refugee camp. I also learned about what she wanted to accomplish in the United States of America.

    Shegitu's story is laid out in this book in compelling detail. Her story stems from her instinct for life as she recounts what it was like living through the Ethiopian Civil War and how she clung to survival by fleeing rape, torture, and death through an Ethiopian diaspora as a refugee in a camp in Nairobi, Kenya, where her son was born. Her story becomes even more personal as she describes the escalating violence in her own home that followed her to the United States.

    Refugee women suffer greatly because of the wars in their homelands. They have lost children, parents, siblings, and husbands. Many have been victims of brutal actions by soldiers and the silence of their neighbors. Some may say that refugee women are victims twice over. As refugees, they are subjected to live as asylum seekers with gashed connections to their native soil. As females, they may fall prey to violence against women and the second-class citizenship that pervades many social contexts.

    Shegitu Kebede, however, is not a victim. Despite the unimaginable hardships she suffered, she refused to victimize herself. Rather, she kept moving in the direction that suited her sense of self while being fueled by her unwavering instinct for life. She possesses an internal power that allows her to see the problems around her and as well as to be a force of change in her own life and in the lives of others.

Shegitu now serves as an advocate for refugee women and their children in Minnesota. She also educates those who are not refugees in hope to inspire them to offer understanding and share resources. As her gripping story unfolds on the pages of this book, she becomes both an advocate and educator for her readers.

- **Jennifer A. Skuza, PhD**

Introduction

  Refugee women are often the poorest of the poor, whether they are "on the run" fleeing danger, have found shelter in a neighboring country, or have been granted asylum in a prosperous country far from their country of origin. They have experienced extreme losses of family, land, possessions, country, and rights. Many have been left alone to raise children and to support the elderly. Women and their children comprise 80 percent of the world's refugees.
  Refugee women are survivors. Often without access to food, shelter, and medical care, they nurture and comfort their families. In the midst of turmoil and deprivation, they gather together. As refugees they are looking for a place to belong. They cry, sing and laugh with each other. "Their instincts are for life," says a male international worker. "The reorientation of life amidst destruction and death comes from women."
  My story is an example of the painful experiences of many third world country women. The list of the countries is long. There is the tragedy Eritrean women and children endured in an ugly war with Ethiopia for more than 35 years. Who can forget the genocide in Uganda? Look at what continues in Sudan after so many years. Somalia still hasn't recovered from its few years of war. Its people are scattered all over the world, leaving the country without a stable government. And this is only one part of Africa.
  The hidden scars of war that so many women from these countries bear are the sources of strength they use to keep on living and caring for their families. Everyone has stories to tell. These are just some of the women's and my own stories. The changes in our lives, our struggles, and overcoming our past are significant to the transformation that we have made. We've found

the confidence to look inside ourselves and each other to find hope.

Our lives are different now. We turned things around from difficult situations and are headed in a new direction. We understand that life sometimes presents us with unexpected or unwanted circumstances we are not prepared for. But no matter what, we recover from these setbacks, and the knowledge and wisdom we gain from them is the source of our personal growth.

Do you ever think about what happens to people after you see the war news on your TV? When a war breaks in any country, it mostly affects women and children. They are weak and vulnerable. Even as they are driven from their homes and family, grieving the loss of loved ones to the war, they have to go on to care for living. They have no time to process their own pain. They have to put their own suffering aside and care for the families and community. You may think the only way people are affected during war is by bombs or war material, but that is not all. It is also the time for rape, torture and for those who take advantage of the weak and vulnerable.

This is the story of my journey through devastation and despair, to hope, healing and wholeness. I am telling my story for several reasons: to inspire other refugee women to be strong and persevere in the struggle to provide the necessities for themselves and others close to them to live; to assist them in finding treatment for the crippling long-term effects of war trauma; and to educate those who are not refugees and inspire them to offer understanding and share resources.

• • •

Hidden Scars

"Women share the twin burdens of violence and inequality."
- Woman from Laos

Refugee women have suffered greatly because of the wars in their homelands. They have lost husbands and children and other family members. They have been forced to leave their homes and all that was familiar and comfortable to them. Many are victims, themselves, of brutal actions by armies, clans, and gangs. Many women are survivors of rape and torture. They have witnessed unspeakable cruelty and endured terror.

Refugee women are victims twice over. As refugees, we are subject to the shared suffering of all who have been forced from their homes by violence. As women, we are vulnerable to incidents of physical abuse, rape, death, the sexual slave trade, and low status.

Despite strong coping skills and the relative material safety offered in the United States, many women resettled in this country continue to suffer because of domestic abuse and the effects of war, and are overwhelmed by the weight of the profoundly different customs and language. The long-term effects of war trauma can be both physical and psychological. Sometimes women feel pain in their bodies or act differently than they did before the war. The symptoms they experience are very often related to the traumatic events they witnessed or personally experienced.

It is my hope that the book will encourage refugee women to seek help for themselves or others, if needed. Often the symptoms of trauma go undiagnosed or are hidden. A strong, cultural stigma about issues of mental illness keep many women from seeking treatment. Shame, cultural restrictions, poverty, and general discomfort in a new environment may prevent them from accessing help. There is strength in knowing that others share the experiences of war and have found resources that assist in the healing process.

· · ·

Visible Strengths

"Women hold up over half the sky".
  - Ethiopian proverb

Refugee women have endured oppression, war, flight, refugee camps, and the hardships of resettlement in a new land and culture. They have faced challenges and losses, but have kept moving forward, caring for their children and other family members. They have relied on their cultural values and faith, beliefs, what remains of their families and communities, and each other to endure. They are rebuilding lives while adding positively to their new, American society.

Storytelling can be a powerful tool for healing. The discovery, in the middle of another's tale, of incidents similar to those of our own lives, reveals to us that we are not alone. Suddenly, we can acknowledge not only our own, but also communal suffering, manage our own pain, and seek out others to give and receive support. Storytelling creates community.

I learned this when I attended a presentation at the Center for Victims of Torture on the distresses and challenges of people from war-torn regions of the world. I felt like someone had told them about me, and they were talking about me in the presentation. This is when I decided to write my own story in my own words.

I was surprised that there were non-refugee Americans who knew something of the experiences of refugees and were deeply concerned for us. I wanted to share this revelation with other refugee women to encourage them as I was encouraged. There is no need to suffer in silence.

Maybe we can understand why refugee women do the things they do or think the way they think. We can ask "why," rather than just brushing them off as newcomers who act strange sometimes. There is nothing in place to evaluate refugees or asylum seekers differently than how Westerners are evaluated, though they have had very different experiences and have different needs. They need help finding treatment for the crippling, long-term effects of the trauma they have witnessed and survived.

There is a demand that women in the marketplace be strong, spiritual, secure, confident, unafraid, influential, and even powerful. As refugee women, these qualities are a result of the pain and hardship we have endured. But sometimes it is hard for us. We need the compassion of those who are not refugees. The slightest sound or gesture can sometimes trigger a painful memory, which causes us to have a mental or emotional setback. We need understanding as we work through these issues and pull ourselves forward to our present reality.

My name is Shegitu, and this is my true story.

My 9th Grade Picture

• • •

My Story

I have fun childhood memories. I grew up with my three brothers, Shuene, Shudamu, and Legide, in a very big compound in the southern part of Ethiopia. There was a school, church, clinic, and boarding area for boys and girls, houses for the missionary, and of course, the orphanage I grew up in. The compound was located between the countryside and the city, so I wasn't living in either the city or the country. It was right in the middle.

All of us orphanage kids

Because there were a lot of kids, we always had fun. We played soccer, volleyball, and basketball, and we gardened, knitted, crocheted, sewed, played board games, and did all kinds of things with the church. We held a raffle to raise money for the church with the things we knitted and crocheted. During the summers, the older students were placed in other hospitals and clinics operated by our church around the southern part of Ethiopia. We volunteered and had many duties that taught us a lot and were also a lot of fun.

My Mom, Dageny

The holidays were the best of all. We performed plays and played all sorts of games, like the three-legged race and hide and seek. We cooked food in our playhouse and had the people who took care of us come and eat, and pay us money for it. We built a lot of playhouses. Those are the fun things I remember from my childhood. Like everything else, those came to an end.

Shegitu Kebede

9

*At the orphanage;
my brothers, the other kids, and me.*

Tea time at home with Mom, Lve.

Two orphanage kids and me (left).

• • •

Ethiopia's Recent History, in Brief

In the early 1970s, the Ethiopian government underwent major changes. Everything changed. The military junta overtook the Emperor Haile Selassie's regime, and established a one-party communist state. Many university students went to the countryside and mobilized the peasantry to prepare for land reforms. Families with more than one home or over a quota of farmland had their land confiscated and were accused of imperialism because the principles of socialism relied on collective ownership. In the city I grew up in the farmers didn't want the land to be taken away, so they started a war. I was in first or second grade, and I had many schoolmates who lost their dads, uncles, brothers and other male family members in this struggle. All men, adolescent to elderly, were forced to fight. The government hunted them down. City men fought against country men just because the city was where the government was located. The government didn't train them properly; there was no time. As a result, countless men were needlessly killed.

By 1976 the EPRP, a party representing the "people's democracy" had eliminated its most obvious, perceived enemies, but two political parties were fighting, and many innocent youth were in the crossfire. It became impossible for any youth not embraced by the Meison party, enforcing a "controlled democracy," to safely walk the streets in his village. More importantly, anyone walking in a group was believed to be "conspiring against the government." The party also required, at gunpoint, attendance at socialist meetings and rallies. People would be severely punished if they didn't show the appropriate level of enthusiasm. The government assigned colors of clothing to denote income levels of its people and also rationed key necessities and supplies. Christianity could not be professed in any way, including wearing a cross on your clothing or walking with a Bible.

University students and faculty were the most outspokenly opposed to the political violence. Many were killed, as were their family members. When the government suspected a person of "wrong-doing," including having held a position with the former government, they would not only kill that person and their family members but also anyone close to them. When the government killed someone, they would take the bodies to a warehouse and make families search through the bodies. When they found their loved one, the government would charge the family for each bullet in the body before they could take it for proper burial.

In 1977, Somalia declared war on Ethiopia, as the nomadic Somalis were fighting to regain the Ogaden area of Somalia for themselves. The Somalis used many weapons from the Soviets, and while the traditional arms supplier of Ethiopia was the U.S., the U.S. didn't assist Ethiopia at this time because it had a socialist government. In the end, the U.S. also funded Somalia because the U.S.'s foreign policy during the Cold War often included helping Communists fight other Communists.

At that point, Ethiopia rejected the U.S. and closed their Embassy. The Soviets saw no contradiction in arming both sides because both were advancing socialism in their own way. Through this violence, the government kidnapped men, young and old, to help fight for their cause.

• • •

How the War Affected Us

My school friend's dad was forced to go to the war. A few weeks later, one of his friends showed up at the family's door with the dad's personal belongings and told them that their dad loved them very much and sent this to them. A few days later she came to school and told us what had happened to her dad. In my simple, childish mind trying to comfort her, I said, "I don't think your dad just died and will never come home. Even if he can't walk, he will roll over the hills and will come home some how." We were surrounded by hills and the war was on the other side of them, so I was pointing to the hill. Even though we were all just little kids, somehow she understood that her dad was not coming home, ever. She said, with tears in her eyes, "No, he is not coming home. He is dead!" I still see her sad face. That was everyday life for the kids at school.

One morning we woke up and wanted to go to school, but the war had escalated, and men with deadly weapons had surrounded the orphanage, using it as a shield. The war was between the New Communist government and the landowners' country men. A few of the country men jumped the fence and used the kitchen to make breakfast, and these soldiers camped right in the orphanage backyard. When the government heard of this, they came to the orphanage to fight the country men.

Many of the orphanage windows were shot out, and we children hid, terrorized, for several days. When it was over, the governor evacuated us out of the city. A military escort accompanied us as we moved to a different missionary compound in a new city. The same day the victorious governor ordered the military escort to protect us he was killed.

The civil war escalated, and there was war in city after city. The government paid money for people to become socialists and many men went against their family values. The war transformed healthy, productive citizens into frightened refugees.

· · ·

The Refugee Flight

People fled the country partly because the government had become dangerously corrupt. People who worked for the government had to do terrible, painful things to their fellow Ethiopians such as throwing them in jail, torture and killing their children. The kidnapping, torture and murder of boys to be soldiers were unbearable. All government officials were known to do these things. Each kept the other's secrets, guaranteeing no blackmail.

The government was scared and struggling, facing wars on all fronts. Civil war against Somalia and against Eritrea, which was fighting for independence from Ethiopia. They were desperate. If they thought you had any information they wanted, they would do anything to get it.

They raped and tortured rampantly. They raped women and girls in front of their fathers or husbands to get the men to talk. They shocked people with electricity or tied them up with a live wire and put them in a bucket of water. Genital cutting, cutting off toes, cutting breasts, gang rapes, and watching one's family members be tortured were common occurrences. The inhumanity was astounding.

Country men and men from small cities were kidnapped from their work or from the market place to be soldiers. These men were not registered as soldiers so there were no benefits or compensation to their families if they were killed. In fact, families were not even informed if they were killed, because to do so would have been an admission of guilt for the kidnapping. Women were terrorized and left with no way to provide for their families, plunging them into poverty.

There was no recourse. To speak out against the government was volunteering to die. One had to pretend to agree with everything the government said or did, even though what was happening was intolerable. People with opposing views, including many people in higher positions and students, were killed or in prison. The poor and low-income men and boys were forced to fight as soldiers. People were desperate. The government arrests got so bad that parents with two sons arrested would go to the prisons and plead with the government to only kill one and give one back. This rarely worked, but it was their last resort. Long-term government workers weren't the only ones; private citizens who ran for local office, once elected, became just as bad as the other government workers.

...

My First Church

Some of our church people also became involved. Though they performed their church duties on Sunday, the rest of the week they behaved like any other officer. I hated the church and thought of its people as the lowest of hypocrites. I started in a direction that was not good or safe for me. I didn't care about anything. Life had no meaning. It didn't matter to me if I lived or died.

The church members' lives did not reflect the Bible they so adamantly preached to us. They treated us roughly, and always said negative things to and about us. They told us that because we were orphans, we would never amount to anything. They called us "Guffy," a derogatory term for orphans, which meant it was our fault we didn't have parents or that we caused our parents' death – that we pushed them away when we were born, and they died. In the view of the church people, we were not whole people because we didn't have parents. Sadly, many of us believed them.

One day, when I was fifteen, someone did something wrong and I got blamed for it. I remember the situation well. I had been hanging out in the girls boarding area of the compound with a few other girls from the orphanage, as well as some of the boarding school girls, and one boarding school boy. I had never met this boy before and I assumed he was one of the other girls boyfriend. Somehow word got back to the head of the orphanage that this boy was my boyfriend, and that I had been sleeping with him.

When the man in charge called us in for questioning I never imagined it would be because I was in trouble for hanging out with these kids. I actually thought he had called us in because one of the women who worked in the orphanage had a relative who had passed away the day before. I thought he was going to ask us to help her out with her chores. Instead, he brought us in and accused me of sleeping with this boy. It didn't matter that I was innocent. He just wanted to make an example of me.

He told us to go out and wait for him by the clothesline. He appeared a minute later with a very big stick. He told the others they could go and then started hitting me. The other orphanage kids were standing on the front porch watching me get beat up by the director. I was bitterly angry. I said to myself over and over, "My heart can cry, but I will not show this man any emotion." I shut myself down completely. I don't know exactly how long he beat me – just that it was for a very long time. I thought over and over that no one deserves to be treated that way. I resolved to leave the orphanage, but I didn't know where to go and what I would do to support myself.

I occupied my thoughts with these questions, and I didn't pay attention to what he was doing. I didn't realize that he was getting angrier because I wasn't crying. He was hitting me faster and harder. He did not want to look like a failure with all the kids watching. After all, he wanted to make me an example of how he disciplined the kids. He was a heavy person, so after hitting me for so long he got tired and was out of breath and sweating, so he could not beat me any longer.

Still, he was cursing me and calling me all kinds of names. I did not feel anything; it was like I was not even there. Afterward, I saw that I was bleeding and bruised all over, but I did not feel any pain at all. Not then. That day was my last day at the orphanage.

I left, just like the other teenagers before me. Like my oldest brother. I had three brothers. Shuene was older and Shudamu and Legide were younger. After Shuene left the orphanage, he was forced to be a soldier and never returned. I still do not know if he is alive or dead.

It was a dangerous time to be alone. At the orphanage, if the military came for the older boys, the orphanage just gave them away. When I left the orphanage, I went to a man I had met a few weeks before. I wanted to marry him so I would have a chance to save myself and my two remaining brothers. I thought, if I had a home I would have a place to hide my brothers. I was determined to protect them, so I married.

This time after I left the orphanage was not easy. There were many times I could have been killed. So many horrible things were happening. I was raped three times. One of these rapes bothers me more than the others because the building I was raped in had very thin walls, and I could hear the people next door very clearly. They did nothing when I screamed and cried out for help. They just continued their conversation, louder and louder. There is no way they didn't hear me.

The situation in our city became more and more unstable, and after a few months, I began my journey to the Kenyan border. My husband was gone on business and I was two months pregnant with his child, but it was not safe to wait any longer.

• • •

My Journey to Kenya

One day I met with some friends to discuss the situation we were in as women. If a man who worked for the government liked you and asked you out, and you refused, they could rape you, put you in jail, or even kill you and get away with it – unless you were an important official's daughter, of course, which none of us were. We knew it wasn't going to get better, and we had to find a way to save ourselves. We knew we would die if we stayed in Ethiopia and we were almost sure we would die if we left – dead either way – so we decided we would die trying to escape. That is how we began our impossibly dangerous journey to Kenya. I left with Wudenesh, a 13 year old boarding student from my orphanage compound. Her family lived on the Kenyan border, so she often traveled there for holidays and summer vacation.

Everyone needed written permission to go from one city to another. Without it, the officials assumed you were trying to escape, and sent you to jail. The police stopped our bus at every small town. I had papers, but I was also trying to escape. I was very scared. In each region there is a distinctive way of dressing, so I dressed up like one of their kinsmen to blend in.

At each stop, an officer would go on top of the bus where the luggage and goods were loaded. He would check everyone's belongings. Illegal things included any produce and coffee, even if you were just taking it from one city to the next. At one stop, one of the officers must have dropped his cigarette up there because almost everything on top of the bus caught fire. Because we couldn't see what was on top of our own bus, we drove on. After quite a while, a military vehicle saw the problem, chased us and made us stop. We had no idea why he did this. During those times, if a military car chased after you, it never ended positively. We were all terrified. Fortunately, on that day, the military was not there to take our lives, but to save them.

When the bus stopped, all the smoke that had been blowing behind came in through the windows, filling the bus. We could hardly breathe. It was hard to get off the bus because there was only one door, but we all made it out. What many of us didn't know was that there was an emergency gas tank on top of the bus, directly above the driver. The only thing between the gas tank and the fire was one large piece of luggage. When the military vehicle stopped us, the soldiers and male passengers helped to stop the fire. Except for that luggage and the gas tank, everything on the bus burned.

Once the fire was out, we were told to continue on our way. We could hardly believe they had just let us go like that. Many of us on the bus were there to run away. We were glad we had dressed up like country people to disguise ourselves.

We continued for three weeks. Three weeks without the chance to wash or brush my teeth. With almost no food and water. Pregnant. It was dangerous to travel during the day because the police were likely to capture us. It was dangerous to travel during the night because the animals might eat us. Between the two, we chose the animals. We traveled at night.

The night we arrived at the Kenyan border we heard that seven of our countrymen had been turned in by the Kenyan police to the Ethiopian police. These people were put in jail for protecting refugees who tried to flee the country. I was staying with Wudenesh's family in the border town where she grew up. Her family told us the Ethiopian police would start beating their new prisoners after a few hours. I was terrified. The hitting began around 9 p.m.

We were across the street from the police station, and my hosts told us to come out of the house to hear the prisoners crying out. Their voices were very loud at first. We could hear them begging the torturers to stop, grown men calling for their mothers, crying out, and screaming. After awhile, it became quieter. Then we didn't hear them anymore. I have no idea how long it took to beat them to death, but it seemed like hours. When it was over, my friend's mother bowed her head and said, "That's it."

I felt like someone had punched me in the stomach. I will never forget her face when she said that. She mourned for these people as if they were her own children. They were someone's babies, and she knew they hadn't done anything wrong. They just believed something different than the government, and had the courage to stand up for their beliefs. She'd heard the same thing every night and grieved for them all. I think her listening and grieving was her way of honoring them.

We had planned to report at the border, but because of what we had heard that night, we changed our plan. We needed someone to take us straight to Nairobi. After a few days, we found a policewoman from Nairobi, and she agreed to take us across the border with her. She told us to come and stay with her, and that we would leave in two or three days. We didn't know it then, but her plan was to make us her servants. We crossed the border and stayed with her for a few days. Both she and her parents had houses there, and she made us do chores in both. She gave us a lot of work to test us, but then told us to go when she saw that my friend was not a hard worker and I was pregnant. On the day we were supposed to leave for Nairobi, her younger brother came to us, and said she had already left without us. We felt betrayed, but at least she had gotten us across the border into Kenya.

Wudenesh was very angry, and said, "We should just return to where we came from, because we could at least have someone to bury us if we are caught and killed." Since her family lived so close to the border, she left and went home. I knew I couldn't do that because I had a much longer way to go. I might make it through one town, but certainly not all of them. After Wudenesh left, I was completely alone. I knew no one, and had no place to go. I had come such a long way and had no home to return to. But I felt encouraged that I had made it across the border and I wasn't about to give up. Earlier, we had met a boy, 11 or 12 years old, who told us how people could successfully cross the border. I went to find him.

He was very kind to me, and clever. He knew all about the border business. He found me a truck driver, who said I should get up in the middle of the night and walk as far as I could away from the border checkpoint. He would pick me up on his way to a different border checkpoint, closer to the Somali border where very few Ethiopians passed through. He said

I should walk near the road but not on the road. He would start on his journey at noon, giving me time to get a good head start.

I got up at 4 a.m. and started walking in the direction he had shown me. I wanted to get out of the town before anyone was awake because the torture I had heard at the border was still fresh in my mind. It was still dark and I was frightened, but I knew this was the best and safest option for me. I had no choice but to trust.

I knew if I got caught I would be turned in to the Ethiopian police, who would torture and then kill me. I walked for hours. My last meal had been the evening before, and I was hungry. I had nothing with me to eat or drink, but just a small backpack with a few extra clothes. I had no idea what I would do or where I would go if I didn't find the driver, but I kept walking anyway. Actually, I knew I would just keep walking if I didn't find the man. What I didn't know was how long it would take for me to die of starvation on my journey. My mind was a whirlwind. Was there a river nearby? If I stopped at a house, would they be kind or turn me in to the authorities? I knew that many people out alone at night were eaten by wild animals. Would I die of dehydration?

I was full of fear, but even though I heard plenty of wild animals and I was at the mercy of this truck driver, I made up my mind to never turn back. That dark walk seemed to go on forever, but finally, I heard honking. When I was sure it was the right driver, I ran to the truck with joy and relief.

The checkpoint was less than a two-hour drive. When we got there, the driver tried to explain to them that I was a student from Nairobi and had been in the border town to visit friends and family. The police asked me for a student I. D. When I was unable to provide it, they tried to talk to me in their language and, of course, I didn't understand what they were saying, and couldn't respond. The policeman got suspicious and sent an armed military escort with us in the truck to the next biggest town where they could arrest and process me. When we got to town the truck driver tried everything he could to get me free, but they said the only way out was to see the judges. Seeing there was nothing more he could do to help me, the driver wished me luck and drove away. He was a nice man. He said he hoped to see me some day in Nairobi.

The guard took me to the police station, said good luck, and left. They put me in a jail cell with many other people, men and women. There was no running water. There was nothing to sit or lie on, other than the bare concrete floor. During the day, the weather was very hot, and I was almost four months pregnant. My entire body hurt, and my neckline was burned so black that my skin was peeling off. In the three weeks I was there I was allowed only one shower. I did not speak their language, and they did not speak mine. The food tasted bad and was very hard to get used to. Some nights it was so crowded that there was no place to lie down. That is how I learned you can fall asleep while you are standing and will not fall down.

I stayed in that overcrowded jail cell for three weeks. No one spoke to me the whole time.

Finally, I was summoned to go before the judge, but he left on a trip before I could be presented. Instead of taking me all the way back to the police station, the guards took me to an actual prison. What a joy! Going to that prison was by far the best thing that happened to me on my journey.

In the prison they gave me my own room and six blankets. I made a nice comfortable bed for myself. I didn't have to sleep on the bare floor as I did in the police station. The food was great, and I was finally able to take a shower and get clean. My blistered skin all came off when I took my first shower, but that luxury was like a dream. After five days it was all over.

I went to see the judge. He had brought in an interpreter just to ensure that I really was Ethiopian and knew my own language. Once he confirmed that, he set me free to go to Nairobi. He also gave me a letter of recommendation to go to the refugee camp. It turned out to be necessary to have this letter when I arrived in Nairobi, and I was very fortunate that the judge gave it to me. The camp officials always asked for it, and if you did not have one, you were required to report back to the border, and the police, to get the letter. By that time, everyone in town was interested in me because they had never heard of an Ethiopian woman coming through the border. They came to meet me, they gave me a place to stay, and they bought me a bus ticket to send me to Nairobi.

Sometimes I look back and see so many things I could not have done by myself. I am grateful. I know I was carried in God's hands through those times.

· · ·

Finding God

When I got to Nairobi I was taken to a temporary home until I went to the refugee camp. Someone invited me to a bible study a few days after I arrived. I'd had a very bad experience with Christianity and religion from my past at the orphanage. I didn't want the same thing again, so I didn't want to go. But they told me, "You have nothing to do. If you go, you will get to know people. Then you won't have to stay here all by yourself." I really had nothing to lose, so I went. The people at the church were specifically reaching out to the new Ethiopian refugees, and were genuinely nice people.

On Sunday I went back to their church, and happened to see a girl from my high school singing in the choir. She was a boarding school girl, and boarding school girls didn't like to be associated with orphanage kids. So I was curious if she was really up there singing and believing, or just going through the motions. After church we met up with each other and reminisced. I saw the changes in her life and the way she was living. She was living a really good Christian life day to day. She was real, and I could see how she had changed for the better from how I had known her back in school. This made me think maybe Christianity wasn't what I had experienced before, but actually a good thing.

After I had been to church quite a few times, I realized the people there were much nicer than those in my home country. Many of the parishioners were wealthy and had good, stable jobs, but they were still genuinely nice to me, as well as to the other poor refugees. Some were business people in Ethiopia, but most of them were not fleeing their country; they were in Kenya working for the United Nations, the Ethiopian Embassy, as pilots, business people, and so on. They didn't need anything from me, but they still wanted me to be a part of their church. I was finally beginning to see a different picture of God, and this is how my attitude and views on God began to change my life.

When I became willing to forgive the people in my life who had caused me to suffer, it put me in fellowship with God. I was ready to be rid of the poison of no forgiveness and bitterness deep within me. It is very hard to forgive another person on your own, but the Holy Spirit empowers us.

Once I got caught up in memories of a person who hurt me badly. I was thinking about him day and night with deep hate and anger. I was so bitter; I couldn't get him out of my mind. It was driving me crazy until one night I got on my knees and prayed for God to help me. I was able to forgive him and forget about him. Without the help of the Holy Spirit, I'm sure this would not have been possible.

We can pray for those who abuse and misuse us, but we can only forgive with the help of God. I prayed for the people in my home country who said they were Christians, but who hurt others and me in so many ways. When we pray for forgiveness, we free ourselves from all that hurt. This realization changed my whole attitude.

Attitude is a choice! We choose how to deal with our circumstances. I once read that life is 10 percent what happens to you and 90 percent how you respond to it. This means that we are more powerful than circumstance. It is up to us to decide how to deal with the events in our lives. If we take this to heart, there is nothing we cannot overcome. God has put what we need in each one of us. It's up to us to choose what kind of attitude we are going to have. It is true that our memory is the only treasure chest we possess, and in it we store the jewels of our past years. But we can decide which memories we'll treasure, and why. We must ask ourselves what kind of jewels we want to possess. I know nothing is impossible unless we say so.

I decided my only goal was to overcome the hate and anger I had been carrying for so long. I realized that God had loved me through it all – even when I was not doing the right thing. He still loves me. The Bible says, "God loves the people of this world so much that he gave his only son so that everyone who has faith in him will have eternal life and never die." I just put my name in it and said, "God loves Shegitu so much." It was like magic.

The realization of God's love for me changed my whole way of thinking. I overcame it all – anger, hate, guilt, resentment. Suddenly it was okay to let it go. I was confident for the first time. I had grown up feeling rejected, unimportant and unwanted. I forgot all of it. What people thought of me was not important anymore because God was there for me. He became the parents I never had. He was anything I wanted Him to be. My mother when I needed a mother, my father when I needed a father, and my friend when I needed a friend. Throughout my life, I have found that when my situation changes, people around me change how they see and treat me. God is not like that. I am so thankful for His unconditional love.

I do not have to compare myself with others. God makes everyone unique with individual skills and talents. In the past, people labeled me. Some said I was worthless because I was an orphan. They put me at a lower level because of my life situation. Now I see that I am not disadvantaged. It really does not matter how people might label me. I am the only person in the whole world like me. One of a kind, made for His purpose. This is a very big thing. It is very deep and personal.

Once I was talking about my past with a friend. I said that God allowed all these bad things to happen to me just to bring me to Him. My friend told me I had it all wrong. God did not allow all that to happen to me. He changed all that happened to me for good. The hard times we go through can teach us to be a better person and to not treat others like we have been treated. I think this is true for everyone, even if they don't know God, because God loved me before I was even slightly aware of Him.

From then on, whenever I had a bad day, I just put God's word before the word of man. I feel courage when I rely on His strength and wisdom above my own. With this change of will and heart, I went to the refugee camp.

• • •

The Refugee Camp

Once I got to the camp I began the process of applying for refugee status. This process usually takes from six to twelve months – sometimes more. There is no way to expedite the process. Besides the one brief interview, there was nothing to do but eat and sleep. We were at the mercy of the decision-makers. We were voiceless and powerless to decide our own future.

Representatives came for interviews once or twice a week, on days that were convenient for them. Even though only a handful of interviewee names were posted each week, we all gathered in front of the office and waited for our name to show up on the list. Like the others, I was interviewed by three people: representatives from the American Embassy, the Kenyan government, and the United Nations. One of them watched body language, one took notes, and the other conducted the interview

The interviewers were not culturally sensitive. In our culture it is not appropriate to look authority figures in the eye. Since, to us these interviewers were authority figures, many of us avoided direct eye contact with them. Because the interviewers were not educated on our culture, they took this as a sign of dishonesty instead of respect. This negativity affected many of the people going through the interviews. This was one of the reasons that many people were not accepted or did not pass the interview. Many people were rejected because of this simple thing, and their lives were deeply affected.

After we were interviewed, we waited nervously for our fate, a life and death situation for every refugee. The reality was that not everyone would make it through the process. This interview would determine if we would receive legal status as a refugee or not. If yes, we would go to our new country and build a new life. If not, we would be turned back out into the nightmare we had just left. I did not think the interviewers knew what it took for us to get there or what it would be like for us if we were turned away. So many of the interviewees were not granted legal refugee status. I don't want to think of what might have happened to them.

I waited a week after the interview to see if I was accepted. There was no announcement. We all had to go every day to the office to find our name on one of two lists: Accepted or Rejected. I was thankful that I was accepted, but some were not. People who were rejected had to pack up and leave in search of another bordering country, another refugee camp, another interview process. We all cried together when people were rejected.

Refugees have no idea what to expect when they set out. The journey is grueling, the heat is overwhelming, they may be dehydrated or hungry, there are many road and animal dangers. They often lose a child, an elder, or spouse along the way. It can take months of walking through the night for them to reach the camp. When they finally apply for refugee status, they think they have reached their goal. But for those who are not accepted, the nightmare journey begins all over again. Except this time, they had no money and no energy left. Some of them never made it. We all grieved deeply for these families because we knew what they had in store. It felt like we were grieving their deaths.

After I was accepted as a refugee, I had to wait to be issued an I.D. card to leave the camp and go to Nairobi. Once refugees obtained their I.D.s, they received some money for basic household items to begin a new life in Nairobi. They must find work to support themselves until they are eligible to ask for asylum in the United States or another country. At the time I was there, we had to wait two years before we could go to an embassy and ask for asylum.

Being a refugee takes a huge amount of stamina. When you are a refugee, you do not have a home or country anymore. You left whatever you owned behind when you suddenly had to run for you life. You never forget that long road you traveled without having enough water or food. If you had a little, you saved it because you did not know how long your trip would be. You can't get rid of those horrible memories of traveling on foot, under cover of night, and the terrifying sound of hungry animals still haunts you years later. But these are not the worst. You left so fast and have been so traumatized yourself that you didn't even have time to grieve for the people you loved. And lost. These emotional scars are deep. I have been in the U.S. for decades and they have not healed yet.

One family's story: the husband was in prison for a long time and they let him out for a little while. The family decided to leave the country before he was imprisoned again. The couple rounded up their three boys and the cash and gold they had at home and went to the Kenyan border. When they got near, they decided to go separate ways for safety and to meet in the Kenyan town that Ethiopian refugees first come to. When the wife got there with her children, she was told that her husband had killed himself. But the autopsy report showed that he was strangled to death because he was carrying a lot of money. I don't know what happened to the wife and her sons.

I didn't escape corruption when I left Ethiopia. The police in Kenya were more corrupt than those in Ethiopia. Refugees think the new country they enter will be safe, but they can never let down their guard. One day my friend went out for a walk on the sidewalk by the refugee camp. Two taxis were competing for business, and were speeding to get to the next stop to pick up more passengers. One driver went onto the sidewalk and hit my friend. She died that day.

I was overwhelmed with joy when I was told I had been accepted as a refugee. There were no words to describe how happy I was. For a refugee such news is truly a gift of life. I know I was not better or smarter than anyone else – but by God's grace I made it through. With that burden lifted, I started thinking more about my pregnancy, the new life that was growing in me. I was determined to give my baby a name that had a good meaning for my life and what this baby would mean to me. I started to pray. A little later, I attended a church service in Nairobi and heard Joseph's story (Genesis 41:51). Joseph called the name of the firstborn Manasseh: For God has made me forget all my toil and all my father's house. I named my child Manasseh.

...

Bringing My Son Into the World

I didn't know if I was going to have a boy or girl, but it did not matter to me. For some reason I just thought that I was going to have a boy. A few months later I went into labor, and the women in the camp warned me to wait until the last minute to go to the hospital. They said the hospital beds were too small, and I would have to share a single bed with another woman, also having her baby. After a long two days of labor, they finally took me to the hospital.

They were right. When I got there, they put me with another woman on a twin-sized bed. It was crowded and uncomfortable. When one of us had a contraction we would wake up the other person. For days I had nothing to eat or drink – not even an I-V. The hospital was a place just to survive. I was physically weak. I was feeling miserable and in a lot of pain, but I remained spiritually strong and felt my faith growing.

After four days of labor I still hadn't had the baby. Finally, the doctor decided I needed to have a cesarean section. He said he was not sure if the baby would be okay.

I knew my baby was fine, and that if there was a problem the Lord would give me the grace to handle it. I placed my baby and myself on the altar just as Abraham did with Isaac. It was up to the Lord if we lived or died. Even so, when they put me in the surgery room, I was scared. I did not have anyone beside me but God.

The miracle happened. My baby boy was born, and he was healthy and beautiful. God had heard my prayers and healed my pain.

The next day I woke up late, and there was nobody around to hear the good news. I knew it was simply because my camp friends had been coming every morning when I had not had the baby. So this morning they were more cautious in showing up. I knew they would be there, slowly but surely.

I was so sore and I was in so much pain that I did not want to share my bed with anyone. Luckily, they did not put me with anyone after surgery, but that night it was raining and some of the windows were open, so I got very cold. I did not have enough blankets and the bed did not have a nurse call button, so there was no way for me to notify the nurse. I was shivering and so cold from head to toe, but when I called out for help there was no one there.

On the third day they took me to another room where I had to share my bed again. This time it was different because it was not only the women in bed, but also the babies. It was just a twin-sized bed for all four of us. The other new mother and I decided that we would sit on each side of the bed and let the babies lie comfortably on the bed.

Although the hospital wanted to keep me for a few more days, it was so hard for me to sit all the time with my stitches, so I requested to go home. They were kind enough to release me back to the refugee camp. They told me to come back in a few days for a check-up on both the baby and me.

In the refugee camp, there was a driver to take us to and from the hospital. The day I went for the check-up, the driver took us to the hospital in the morning, but was nowhere to be found for our return trip a few hours later. We waited all day, with no comfortable place to sit, lie down or lay my baby down. I was weak and in pain because I still had stitches from my c-section, so my friend held my baby. We did not have money to take the bus or for food or water. Around five or six p.m., before the sun went down, we saw that we would have to walk back to refugee camp – a four-hour walk. Otherwise we had no place to stay.

After two hours of walking in the dark, someone stopped their car for us and was able to drive us the rest of the way. When I returned to camp, I realized my stitches had opened and I was bleeding. My white dress was covered in blood. I had been too exhausted to notice it while we were walking in the dark. I did not know what to do. My friends ran and got one of the refugee women who had been a nurse back home, and she came and took care of me. She saw that my stitches had opened, found a driver, and sent me back to the hospital.

Gradually, through all my trials, I became emaciated and weakened. But I was also blessed with the women in the camp, who helped me with my daily life. I had little to no worries while I was healing. They knew it was not easy to be a teenage mother, and I had a lot to learn. They were very patient, and always there to teach me. I am still so grateful for those friends. Slowly but surely, I grew stronger. I drew comfort from God, and felt encouraged to find the strength to do everything that needed to be done.

Eventually, the time came for us to leave the refugee camp. It was hard to go after having lived in the camp. Even though things weren't always great, I had learned to manage there. The camp had become my home and community. I could not even imagine how our lives might turn out. This time, though, I didn't feel so alone. God was with my tiny family, and we would be fine. We would take just one day at a time.

• • •

Finding Solace in God

All my life I had felt unloved and unwanted, and I had stopped caring about anything. But God wants us to care for each other and ourselves. When I understood this, I changed my attitude and found new issues to deal with, including my parents' deaths. When I was little, I was happy with my missionary caregivers, but by the time I was old enough to question who I was and where I came from, the country was at war and people in my life had become hard and mean. There was a lot of killing. As a teenager I was too filled with hate and anger to reflect on the fundamental questions of my life.

Many refugees became Christians when we felt our lives were empty and meaningless. We needed something we could hold onto. God became my father, mother, husband and best friend, so I was not alone. Finally, with peace in my heart, I was able to focus on and process the events of my life and my family's deaths. I knew I would be able to find the faith I needed to overcome these difficult times and become the person God intended me to be. But most of all, I could rest. I could do what I needed to do with a peaceful heart.

I have always been able to find compassion for hurting, broken-hearted people like me. The harder part was to forgive the resentment I felt against anyone who had harmed me or others. I learned that we must overcome evil with good. That takes a lot of strength, but it's the only way. I am still so grateful that I found a deeply connected and loyal family in the fellowship at my church.

With so much time on our hands at the refugee camps, many people started to have mental health issues. Finding God helped them keep their sanity. We wanted to heal and live a good and honorable life.

Coming to know God does not change everything overnight. Knowing God does not mean I will have a problem-free life, but it is comforting to know that He will provide the strength and wisdom to deal with whatever problems may arise. It means that I am healed from the inside out and that I have the strength to do the work that needs to be done. Since then, most of our lives have improved drastically, and our finest dreams have begun to take shape. God has been faithful to us. He has brought us so far.

Getting ready for overnight prayer in Nairobi, Kenya.

• • •

Settling in Nairobi

It was time to heal these things hidden inside of me for so long. There was a lot of dealing with my past spiritual and emotional issues. I needed to address all of my issues for me to be able to move forward. I knew I needed to start from deep down inside and reconcile one thing at a time. To find energy for this, I needed to set some personal goals. I had to ask myself what kind of woman I wanted to be and what my plan would be to accomplish that.

With church friends in Mombasa.

The UN gives official refugees a small amount of money when they leave refugee camp to start a new life. I was able to find an apartment in Nairobi and get a few basic things with this money. Then I received a scholarship for school. I knew God wanted me to benefit from my past; he gave my baby and me people who loved and cared for us. And I became reacquainted in Nairobi with some people from the church where I grew up. Thankfully, these were not the same people who had done so much to hurt me.

Some people from the church provided everything we needed to improve our lives. I put my son in day care and went to school. We were very fortunate to have so many good people in our lives. Nairobi was changing rapidly, and things got very expensive. But God was faithful to us. There were times when I did not have any money, but my son was not hard on me. When I did not have money for milk he was content to drink water. There were times when we did not have any food. Whatever I had he was willing to take and never complained. This was one way that God was providing for me. God's blessings come in many ways, through agreeable children, providing people in our lives, giving us strength, making new resources available to us, and so on.

There was a hard time when I couldn't finish work early enough to pick up my son from his day care on time. I left work early enough – the problem was transportation. People who used public transportation in Ethiopia always gave up their seats for elders and women. They also gave them the opportunity to get on the bus first when arriving at the stop. This wasn't the case in Kenya. There were always more people waiting for the buses than there was room on them. The strongest and most energetic got on the buses first. The elderly, weak, and disabled were left behind. I was weak and could never get on the first buses, thus I could never get to pick up my son on time. The day care had warned me many times that they could not keep my son so late. The last time they told me that, my son could not come to them anymore.

I was so frustrated and angry. Because of that, I was not able to work for four months and we did not have any money. The area we lived in was very expensive, so I needed to move. The landlady gave me one week to move out because she needed to house her new maid in the servant quarters, which I had been renting. Miraculously, at the same time, a friend from church had to leave for Australia unexpectedly. He had prepaid his rent three months in advance so I was able to stay in his home. Through another turn of events, I ended up not needing to pay rent the entire time I stayed there.

This was another way that God blessed us. Suddenly I felt I understood the world and more of life just because of my little experiences. I learned things do not always work the way we plan, but they will work out. I think the challenges and difficulties in the process are what make our lives interesting and help us to realize that we are the source of our own growth. Life, like any game, needs to be played. The only ones safe in the game of life are the spectators, those who do not play at all. They may miss the danger, but they also miss the meaning and joy.

Me, as a bridesmaid (last on right).

When one door closes, God will open another one. I was invited to be a bridesmaid in a friend's wedding, but was penniless and jobless at that time. The bridesmaids planned and coordinated the entire wedding and worked at the bride's home every day for two or three weeks before the wedding day. I didn't know how to tell the bride that I didn't have any money, especially because we lived on opposite sides of the city, and it took all I had to pay the fare from one side to the other every day. I was thinking about this one day before church and was overwhelmed at the thought of it. Afterward, another bridesmaid reminded me that in the evening we had to go to the bride's house to begin the wedding planning. I was so worried about it that I just opened up to her.

I told her I couldn't afford the trip fares. She told me that her fiancé had come from Australia and had given her some money to prepare for her trip to Australia. She had an extra $100 that she didn't know what to do with. She said that she had prayed about how she should use the money, and God said that she should walk out that morning with the money and she would find someone who could use it. When I told her about my situation, she knew I was the person God was leading her to. She handed me the money.

When I got to the bride's house, I was assigned to work with the pastor's wife. I had been in the choir with her for more than two years, but we had never had a personal conversation. While we were planning our tasks for the weeks ahead, she abruptly stopped and asked me how my personal life was going. I told her about my frustrations with no job and no money and also the story about my friend who had just given me that money. She got up, went to her bedroom and came out with more money for me. She passed the information around the church, and soon one of the members contacted me because he was looking for a female voice for the radio. He and a friend came to my house to ask me if I wanted the job on the radio station, and I was hired on the spot. God blessed me in so many ways to help me survive until I came to America. Since that day, I have never lost a job.

I enjoyed my job and, at the same time, learned from it. I worked in a Christian radio station very close to my home and my son's day care so we did not need public transportation anymore. While I worked there

I got an opportunity to travel to the United States. God works mysteriously. He always knows what is good for us, and He only has the best ways for us when we trust Him. He always gives us the desire of our heart.

At the time, once refugees were accepted and had moved to Nairobi, they had to wait two years before applying for asylum at one of the foreign embassies that were accepting refugees. After two years, I went to the U.S. Embassy and applied for asylum. I was called for an interview and after waiting three months for the results, I learned I was not accepted. Dissatisfied with the result, I asked for an appeal, and, miraculously, the second time was successful. After I was accepted, the U.S. Embassy gave me a voucher to go to one of their clinics for a physical exam. I knew they were looking for tuberculosis, HIV or any other chronic disease. When the results came back I again found my name posted on a list for people who passed.

Next I was sent to the International Office for Migration (IOM) where I met with people who would find me a sponsor in the U.S. They found one for me through churches in Fargo, North Dakota, but I had to wait for them to find me a flight. This took a full year because the IOM only finds empty seats on commercial flights and fills them as space and destination allow. I always had to go to their office to see if I had made the flights list. When my name finally appeared on the list, they got me a passport and took care of my visas. The IOM even took care of me and all refugees going through their service at the airport and on layovers. My final destination was Fargo, North Dakota.

Life in Kenya, (third from right).

• • •

White America

When I arrived in North Dakota, it was mid-November, cold and white. I had never seen snow before. And I was afraid I would never see grass again. I actually wrote to my friends and told them the United States did not have grass or leaves. The snow was piled up to the second and third stories of buildings. We did not know how to dress for cold weather. At first we did not even have proper clothing. But our sponsors gave us all the clothing we needed. Next came the challenge of dressing my son for every five-minute outing. That was challenging.

Time passed and winter changed, as did everything else. The day we got to the United States our sponsors had a dinner planned with an Eritrean family. They had prepared a traditional Ethiopian/Eritrean dinner so we would feel at home. I really appreciated that very much. We became good friends, and a few months later her brothers and their families arrived in North Dakota, as did a Somali woman and her son. Finally, there were a few more East Africans in Fargo! We all got busy going to school and work.

There were a few churches in Fargo that sponsored us, including the Episcopalian, Presbyterian, and Catholic Churches. Five women from these churches helped my son and me when we came to Fargo. They were the nicest people I had ever met. Each had a different assignment, and they took me grocery shopping, furnished my apartment, and whenever we needed them they were there. We also met a few other wonderful women from Fargo: Gloria, Kitty and Cody. They touched our lives forever. We will never forget what they did to make our lives better.

We stayed in Fargo for half a year. At first I worked in a nursing home. Then someone found me a job in a factory, where I worked part-time and took English language classes part-time. We were very lonely in

Fargo, but we met an Ethiopian/Iranian couple who invited us over, and we found a group of African and African-American college students to celebrate holidays with. We were delighted about this since there were very few Africans and African Americans in Fargo.

My son celebrated his fourth birthday in North Dakota. I was lonely most of the time, even though my sponsors would help when they could. It was a very difficult time. In our culture people are always friendly with their neighbors. They never close their door during the daytime. This means that any one from the neighborhood can come in and visit. If a new person moved to the neighborhood, everyone came to meet them and spend some time with them. They would show the new person around and made sure they would never be lonely. It wasn't the same in Fargo. I was lonely and I needed someone to talk to every day, but there was no one. I still remember the first movie that gave me a good laugh after three or four months living in the U.S. Finally, a few more refugee families came and we knew we had places to go and people we could visit.

When spring came, I was so happy to see the sun and the warm weather. All the snow melted away as fast as it had come down. We ventured out to the parks and malls and just started having fun. I thought my life had just begun, but I was about to face a major grief.

• • •

Bad News

    Writing about my brothers has seemed to hold me back. I have done so many difficult things in my life, but writing this book has become very challenging in a new way. There are people and events I still cannot bear to elaborate on. I cry a lot – the loss is so real and so deep. I could not have imagined this when I began, but now I see that these wounds are still very fresh. Maybe they always will be, but I believe I must face this. Writing about my brothers can help me heal and might somehow help others who may be facing these same kinds of challenges.

    One sunny afternoon in 1990, I went down from my third floor apartment to check my mail. I noticed the distinctive envelope from Ethiopia. I was so excited to read it that I just sat on the steps in front of the mailboxes and opened it. But what I found was not something I was prepared to know. I felt like someone had punched me in the stomach. It was from a friend back home. She said that my middle brother, Shudamu, had been killed. Also, my younger brother, Legide, had been forced from a public bus and sent to war. I felt sick. I was not sure if I was sitting or standing and I could have sworn the ground was moving under me.

    I thought of the stories I heard in the refugee camp about what the soldiers go through in war. One of the stories that stuck in my mind was how soldiers were forced to fight. Most new soldiers were young boys who had been kidnapped. Members of the military would not train these boys but would throw them straight into battle. The new soldiers couldn't back away because their commanders were behind them with guns aimed at their backs. Either the enemy or their own men would kill them. No one stopped to notice if they were killed. There were no letters written to families or friends. The dead were simply forgotten as the fighting went on around them. I tried to imagine what must have gone through Legide's mind; he was just fifteen. Was he still alive? Was he suffering? Just when I was starting to find a place in the world again, I felt lost.

My world turned over. I didn't know what to do. I had no one to turn to except my four-year-old son, and he had no idea what was going on. In my crazed state, I picked up the phone and called everyone I knew. I thought everyone felt the same way I did. I know I have been saying that we can grow from the bumps in the road of life; but even after all of the bumps in my life, I was not ready for this. I didn't know how to grieve. I convinced myself that if I had been there things would have been better for my brothers. It was so hard to be strong and go on with my life after losing my beloved brother, Shudamu. And the uncertainty of Legide's situation was too much. I was confused and very lonely. I was full of regrets.

After I read that letter, my happiness was gone. I thought I'd never be happy and smile again. The heaviness in my heart was overwhelming. I couldn't find any place in my soul to rest. My dreams were scattered by this new reality. I had been planning to bring my brothers to the States after I settled down. Now, suddenly, everything was different.

Even though in my country I had seen many people get killed, this was the first time as an adult that I had to deal with the death of someone very close to me. I was completely lost. I thought I would never get over it and that there was nothing left in me to go on. My brothers were the only blood relatives I knew.

That night I could not sleep, so I talked with God. I poured out my heart to Him. I cried out my deepest sorrows and sensed that He was walking me step by step through my grief. He also sent two wonderful women to spend time with me: Elizabeth and Brooke. The next day these ladies came and stayed with me. I had met Elizabeth earlier, and she came from Minneapolis after I phoned her. They prayed with me and were there to comfort me all night. My sponsors had never met my brother. They gave him a great memorial service, which comforted me. I will never forget those generous people. I pray that God will comfort them and be with them all their days.

After I received the letter from my friend, my sponsors and I tried everything we could to get my little brother back from the war. We appealed to the government, by the Geneva Convention, stating that only one member in a family should have to fight in a war. We informed the International Red Cross, but we were unsuccessful. I made a choice to trust God completely and prayed for Legide's safety. A few months later the government changed and the war with Eritrea ended. Legide was free.

He was free from the war, but not from loneliness and depression. Legide had never known our parents, and when he was a child, our oldest brother, Shuene, had been taken and never seen again. Legide had been just a little boy when I left the country. Now his other brother, Shudamu, had been killed. He was just fourteen, with no one to turn to and no place to go. The orphanage where we had grown up told him they had no place for him anymore. He was homeless and begged for food on the street. When that did not work, he stole and sold the goods for food. He started drinking, doing drugs, smoking cigarettes, and rummaging through people's trash for food. When a person no longer cares about anything, it's easy for them to live this kind of life.

Finally, two years later, we were able to connect with each other by phone through friends in Ethiopia. But it was too late for me to help my brother. My friends who still had contact with him told me there was nothing left for me to do to save him. They said it was a waste of money whenever I sent anything to him. I sent him a suitcase of clothes, but it did not even last for a month. He sold the clothes to buy drinks and drugs, and when I sent money he would use it for his bad habits. A week later he would be broke again. I did not know what to do for him. I went through so many people to get help for Legide. Each one of them said that there was no hope for him and advised me not to invest anything more in him.

Legide was silently screaming for love and compassion and rejecting it at the same time. It was so painful for me to watch my only brother go downhill like this. I felt powerless and hopeless, but I could not just give up on him. I loved him and cared about him very deeply. If I gave up on him, who would still care?

I cried out to God every day about Legide. I know God does not see in the same way people see. He sees the good where people can only see faults. Sometimes it is hard to see in the moment that God can take all this confusion and struggle and cause it to fade away. I needed answers and help. I wanted to know where God was. I said, "God, help me to hold on. I know you have a purpose for our life in this world. I need your help now." I know He was listening.

After six years of struggles, Legide finally called to tell me things had turned around for him. His voice was different. We had talked a lot on the phone before that, but usually when we talked he made up outrageous lies to get money. This time it was so different; there was calmness, delight and joy in his voice. Legide had found his way to God.

• • •

Reuniting

Several years later I was able to go to Ethiopia for one month to see Legide. We never left each other's side the whole time I was there. We cried and laughed together, and also talked about our past and what life has been for us since we were separated. The first time seeing each other after so many years was surprising. We had both aged a lot. And looked very different than when we had last seen each other. We laughed at our failures, complimented each other's successes, reminisced about our childhood together and marveled at the way God has seen us through it all. We also met with other orphanage kids we grew up with and with our missionary mother, Liv. We played all the games we had played as children. It was good to see everyone and catch up on what they were doing and find out what was going on in their lives. I didn't get much rest while I was there, but it was one of the greatest times in my life.

I could see that Legide had been carrying a lot of resentment about our brother Shudamu's death. He was bitter toward the people who caused Shudamu's death, and toward the church. He said that when Shudamu died, the church decided he had not been a good person or, at least, not a good church member, so they did not hold a funeral service for him. That hurt Legide deeply. I told him that I believed what we do or don't do for the deceased person is not important. It does not make any difference to the dead. I said, "Who cares about what the church does after Shudamu is dead? They weren't nice to him when he was alive either. If we want to make a difference, we need to do it when the person is alive." I told Legide about the unforgettable memorial service my new friends and sponsors in North Dakota had given in Shudamu's honor. That gave Legide great relief.

When I first learned of everything that had happened to my brothers I struggled with feelings of guilt and sadness. I was obsessed with "what ifs," and I could not think clearly. There was nothing I could have done to change the circumstances, and I was angry at my powerlessness. My faith had taught me to control my thoughts and behavior, but self-control and forgiveness were not the first things that came to my mind. It is hard to understand why people do what they do or think how they think until we have a chance to deal with troubles like theirs. The powerful lesson that I have learned about dealing with crisis and tragedy is that I cannot change the circumstances, and there is nothing I can do to prevent them, either. However, even though feeling angry is normal, acting on my anger is not the best thing I can do.

It is hard to look back on what happened in my homeland and in the refugee camps and to forgive those who hurt my loved ones and me. But no matter how much it hurts, I have to forgive and ask for forgiveness also. That is a source of strength. You may not be ready to forgive, but it's important to release anyone who caused you hurt and get it out of your heart. After that, your own healing can begin.

Forgiveness was possible for me because I believed in the goodness of God and myself, not because someone was telling me, "You can do it!" Otherwise, if I accepted how society labels people in my situation, then I would say to myself: I'm black and an immigrant with limited English, and to make matters worse I'm an orphan. I would have failed. I'm not willing to let any of the tragic events in my life become a hindrance in fulfilling my God-given destiny.

Excuses can stop us from discovering our victory! Getting through tough times is not easy, but we won't be helping anything by getting angry with others or ourselves. It's good to remember we're not alone. Other people overcome difficult things in their lives as well. When I first came to this country, it was cold. I hate cold and snow everywhere! But I thought about the people who came to this country before all of us, before furnaces and snow removal systems, without comfortable houses and warm clothing, without all these inventions we have now. Yet they endured all of this to make life better for themselves and the people who would come after them.

Positive attitude is the most important thing in a person's life. The

Bible talks about David facing a giant. When David faced his giant, he did not have any supporters or any one to cheer him on. His brothers thought he was out of his mind and out of his place. He did not belong there; he was weak and too young. The King and his people were thinking the same thing, but they did not have anyone else who was brave enough to face the giant, so they let David do it.

The giant looked down at him and said, "From what I can see, you are not experienced. You have no idea what a warrior looks like. You do not look like one, so please go home before you bring shame to your family's name. You do not have the right weapon. You do not look like you have ever been in combat, and you do not have a fan club like I do. Let me show you what a real warrior looks like and does."

Through all of that David stayed focused, did what was in his heart, and was victorious. Whenever I read David's story, I say to myself, we all have our own giant to face at times in our life. It could be health, marriage, career, family or finances. But whatever it is, we should face it without focusing on our circumstance, but on our inner strength. That is what David did to overcome his giant.

When I was growing up I did not have anyone to tell me they loved me, to encourage me or ensure my safety. Everyone thought that given my circumstances, I would become a junkie. Remember, people's opinions should never impact who you are! You are the only one who can define your destiny, and it is important to understand that power. There's a lesson for each of us to learn and specific things we have to do to follow a set of plans and goals to change our life.

If I could only change one thing about my past life experience, it would be to worry less and enjoy the things that matter more. For many years I did not enjoy the beautiful seasonal changes that the Midwest presents. It was like I was in a locked cell. Then I was diagnosed with low back problems, and that turned my life upside down. Pain makes you see things differently. I thought about my life very deeply, and my focus and priorities started to change. I started to see the structure of my life, and not just what was currently happening. I became more positive. The things that used to bother me were not such big issues any more. I dealt with things differently and felt different about them. Why wait for some traumatic event to happen before we reevaluate life?

...

Abuse

I also had to deal with the dark secret I had been living. The secret that was melting me away. The ancient secret of domestic abuse. My husband was addicted to violence.

The first time it happened I was coming home from my first job in my new city. My husband had been in the U. S. for just a few months. It had only been a little while since we had been reunited after four years in different countries. He was at my friend's house with her husband and our kids. My friend and I worked at the same place. My husband had tried the same job I had, but he quit. I was grateful just to have a job.

In those days not everyone had a car, so I was giving rides to my friends who worked with me. After work I would give two of them a ride home since we all lived on the same street. That particular day I called my husband before I left work to let him know I was on my way to pick up him and our five year old son. I guess he thought I took longer than I should have to get to him.

As soon as we got there, my friend and I got out of the car and went in the building. My husband was furious! He demanded to know why it had taken me so long. When I told him that I was dropping off my male coworker, he began to call me names. He accused me of messing around with my coworker. It did not matter to him there were two women in the car with our male coworker. He had convinced himself that I was fooling around with my coworker while he was waiting for me.

I can still see that angry face and hear how he slammed the door as he dragged me out to the car. He drove way too fast and sped through stop lights. He swerved dangerously past other cars. I was afraid we would all die. My husband was cursing and yelling at me. I was begging him to let us out. I had one hand on the back seat, holding my son's legs to comfort him, and the other hand on the door hanging on for dear life. I was terrified. I had never seen someone that angry in my life. I think that is the day he told himself, "I've got this right where I want her." After that day, physical violence was a daily routine.

When I was in this abusive situation, my energy was not used to create and achieve life goals and plans. It was all wasted on hopeless wishing. There was no seeking counsel – I couldn't even hear my own voice. Everything was dark and negative. I wondered if there was more to life than what I knew. And I was afraid of what could happen if I managed to get out of that abusive life or what my family or friends would say. Those are the things that held me back. Most immigrants and refugees consider what the community will say rather than what is good for us as individuals.

That empty life took all my energy, spent my emotions, and did not allow space to think clearly or be productive. I was stuck. My life was full of wishes, like many women in my country and women all over the world who are stuck in domestic abuse. I gave up and told myself, "This is your life. Just live it. Or maybe just ignore it and it will go away." But it did not go away. The abuse I experienced was deeply controlling verbal, emotional and physical abuse. Instead of going away, it got worse and worse. It became every day life.

Making a decision in our community requires consultation with our extended family. For those of us who do not have an extended family or have been separated from them, this, in itself, is a challenging barrier to change. It causes ongoing depression and a lot of anxiety.

My old neighbors would say, "We knew something was wrong with you. You did not associate with anyone closely. You were shy, quiet and kept everything to yourself. You are young, beautiful, smart, and wise. How could you let something like this happen to you?" To tell you the truth, I don't know and I'm still asking myself the same question.

I know I was afraid, made a lot of excuses for myself, and felt powerless, even though I knew it was wrong that my children and I were treated as we were. I told myself that if I took them away, I would not be able to provide for them as they were used to. Since I knew what it was like not to have a home, it was very important for me that my children did have one. I did not know then that I could make my husband leave. And I did not know that I was not thinking clearly. I can see now that I was only thinking about their physical needs.

    I became completely isolated and depressed and I did not know how to change it. Most of the time my husband was angry, and I never knew why. When he got home, instead of enjoying his family, he would look for something wrong that he could get angry about. He had no eyes to see anything good. He called us names and cursed us. When not satisfied with that, he would start hitting.

    I never knew how much money we had. He would take my paychecks, sit down and scrutinize them. He would make me go back to my Human Resources department at my place of employment and say they cheated me an hour. He was that much in control. He made sure I was distanced from people so they couldn't figure out what was going on in our home. I was a prisoner in my own life. I was like a thick pillar candle. When you burn it down to the bottom, the outside of the candle holds its form, even though it is hollow inside. That was my life.

• • •

Back Pain

On top of it all, I was suffering from terrible lower back pain. I felt broken and useless. What I needed was loving support and encouragement, but the way my husband treated me made it clear that I was an unbearable burden to him. I went into a deep depression because of my broken way of life and the physical pain. For two years I wasn't able to work. During those years, being house-bound, I don't remember one day that he was kind toward me. But he often called from work to complain if I was still in bed. He demanded that food be on the table when he came home. My back felt worse and worse.

This was a repeat of my childhood in Ethiopia. When people didn't do as they were told, they were tortured or killed. It was not much different in my own home. Because of how I was treated, I thought I really wasn't doing things right and that I was a bad person. I began to believe the things my husband said. I felt stupid. Now I regret that a lot because I can see the effect it has had on my children. I can see how much it took out of them.

I quickly saw how easy it was to just waste away. I realized that if I didn't do something about my life, no one else would do it for me. Once I understood this, I stopped caring what others might think or say. I did not care for the traditional, unrealistic advice. I was determined to go strongly in the direction of freedom. No more wishful thinking. I knew deep down that if I needed something I would have to make a way for it to happen.

A nice couple lived in the apartment above ours. I became good friends with them, and they came down from time to time and took care of me, cooked for me, and did what I needed around the house. They couldn't believe what my marriage was like.

One day I went to the doctor for a spinal tap. It was so painful, I could hardly move. I called my husband and told him I was in a lot of pain. I asked him to bring home some food for the children and me because I couldn't move. He brought Chinese food, threw it on the table, and demanded, "Will you at least serve it?" My neighbors had been there all day to help reposition me from one side to the other. They could not believe what they were witnessing, but this was a daily occurrence for me. My husband was sure I was exaggerating to the doctors. He thought I should get better right away. I wanted that too. But that did not happen.

No matter how much I tried, I could not see the light at the end of the tunnel. I was emotionally emaciated and deeply depressed. One morning I looked out the window and saw leafless trees that looked dry and gray. It just hit me: that was how I felt. That was what my life looked like. I wanted to end my misery, but could find no help. I thought the only solution was suicide.

I decided to do it after I sent my kids off to school. I filled up the bathtub, got a glass of water and six or seven different pain pills, and stepped into the water. I put all the pills in one cup in case it did not work right away. If someone found me passed out, I did not want them to know what kind of pills I had taken. I didn't want to be rescued. I was prepared to die.

I put the first pill in my mouth, but as I lifted the glass of water, I thought of my children. I thought I heard some voice saying to me, "What kind of example are you leaving behind for your children?" I pictured what it would be like for my children to find me dead in the bathtub. My children always got home before my husband, and I knew that they would open the door and call, "Mom, we're home!" And if they did not hear my voice, they would come to my bedroom to wake me up. They would be devastated to find me dead. That hit me hard. It was selfish of me to think only of my own pain. I no longer wanted to die.

In the struggles, pain, and disappointment, I was so focused on my problems that the situation almost destroyed my strength. Instead of me squeezing life out of my situation, my situation almost squeezed the life out of me. To the core of my being, I knew I wanted a different life, but I did not know how to find or create it. I wanted to live a life of integrity. I now see how easy it is to be overtaken by a problem when a decision needs to be made. I'm so grateful to God, who shook off my impossibilities and gave me strength to make a new beginning. He spared my life that day, I'm sure.

Life is precious, even in the worst of circumstances. The way I had responded to my circumstances didn't hold up to the integrity I wanted in my life. No one should take life for granted. I recognize today I almost denied myself the chance to be part of my children's graduations from elementary school, high school and college. I would have missed weddings and grandchildren. God loves to bless us with all these things. I look back at when God helped me to look into my blind spot and to see how my kids have turned out to be beautiful and productive people. It gives me chills deep in my bones to think that I almost messed it all up.

• • •

Healing the Pain

I worshipped with the American church, but one day a friend invited me to go to an Ethiopian church with her. The guest was a well-known pastor from Ethiopia, Daniel Mekonne. During the service he called out to all who were sick or suffering. When he called my condition I went forward. He prayed for me and gave me a word from the Bible. I did not get better right way, but from that time I applied the word of God that he gave me. I was so committed to my own healing that I went back to work. Even though I still suffered I was no longer consumed by the pain. Instead, I worked through it and did everything the job required.

Faith is not what we can see, but what we do when we envision what we want to happen. Life does not always serve us what we want. Even so, despite our situation, we can expect great things in our future. I have learned that the quickest way to change my circumstances is to have a humble attitude.

The pain lessened, but I was still emotionally paralyzed from the abuse and it was getting worse. I started working longer hours, including weekends and holidays, just to avoid being home with my husband. When I was home I tried to do everything I could around the house to avoid criticism. But it didn't work. Plus, I felt guilty because I was not home with my kids.

I had seen the effects of my husband's violent behavior on my children, especially on my son. He was beaten every day before he went to school. In his father's eyes he wasn't brushing his teeth fast enough, or getting ready quickly enough, or anything else that could be an excuse for brutality. He became very shy and withdrawn and would not talk. His childhood happiness was stolen from him. This hardship my kids and I were going through was too much.

I even struggled with day care because I was working such long hours. When I took my daughter to the baby-sitter, people thought I wasn't a good mom and I didn't care about her. One time I took her to the baby-sitter even though she had a bad cold. It was my husband's day off, but he refused to take care of her and I had to go to work. The sitter's family almost called the police on me. But there is light at the end of even the longest tunnel. Eventually, God provided someone who could truly love my baby daughter and care for her like her own child. Today her family is part of our family.

I knew I must live purposefully, contributing to life, but my own emptiness was overwhelming. My marriage was costing me my life. I was not afraid to die; in my opinion, I was not alive anyway. All this time I had been looking for answers from the outside, but I realized the answers were all within me. I reached in deep for them. Nothing is worth more than having freedom and peace of mind.

When I set goals for my life, I know I must be willing to do whatever it takes to overcome the obstacles on my path. I knew that if I did not want my brokenness and sorrow to follow me, I would have to leave it behind and keep remembering the difference between hopelessness and a life of purpose. I see all the things that have happened in my life as steppingstones. Getting through them has been like training to build strength and endurance. I'm strong enough to empty myself of those memories and the constant fear of being overwhelmed by life's impossibilities.

When we look at an athlete's lifestyle, they are ordinary people trained for special projects. Those athletes go through so much training before they actually do the real thing. I believe God has something special in my life plan, so he is using the things I went through for my own good – even the mistakes that I made. I have also learned that if a person does not first wish and then have plans to work with, he or she cannot achieve anything. With everything in life, there is always hard work. Today I am drawing plans and establishing goals one at a time.

I grew up hearing people around me say I wouldn't amount to anything because I was just an orphan. They wouldn't want their kids to hang out and play with me because I was a nobody in their mind. Now, when I see people in that situation, I know how to deal with it. I have been there and know how it feels. My experience has helped to open my heart.

∙ ∙ ∙

Staying Strong

A few days after my bathtub near-suicide, my husband hit me so badly that I was bruised all over. I fled upstairs to my friends' place. They could not believe that I let this happen to me, but they did not know what to do with me, or in what way they could help me. They suggested I could stay in a shelter. I called, but that day they were all full, so I went back home again. My friends were so upset, but I didn't know where to go. My husband took all the money I earned and I had no access to it. I couldn't go to a hotel or anywhere else without getting money from my husband.

This pattern became established. Every time my husband beat me, my children and I would go to a shelter. He would search for us and beg us to come home again. He even brought his aunt from Chicago to help him. He always called me stupid, and I began to think maybe I was stupid because I kept putting up with him. But in my mind, I told him over and over, "I'm not stupid. If you mistake my concern for my children for stupidity, then you are stupid. I'll show you." And I began my work.

One time his aunt was visiting with us and said to me, "Our family has talked about your situation. If my nephew hits you again, you tell me. He will need to leave you. You aren't at fault. We know what you are going through. You have no reason to leave your home. If he doesn't listen, call the police and let them get him out."

The next time he beat me, I told him to leave. He wasn't worried because his family had always backed him up before. But this time they told him he was on his own, and no one came to his rescue. In his desperation, he made a lot of threats, and almost strangled me. But life or death, I made up my mind I was going to leave that life behind. He put me through so many problems, but I stuck to my plan. I knew this time I'd had enough. I knew it was not going to be easy, but God was on my side.

To hurt me, my husband made up stories that I was sleeping with rich white men and that I had neglected my children. I told myself it did not matter what others thought of me. This is my life and I need to do what is right for my kids and myself. But my husband convinced my son to believe the lies. For a year and a half my son and I didn't speak much. Our conversation was not more than hello and goodbye. I held on and prayed that my son would come around to see the truth. My son moved in with his dad. My daughter and I lived together for that year. I knew I needed to be patient with my son because he was going through so many things. My ex-husband was good at making people believe things, so I knew it was going to take time. Sooner or later, who we are will surface. Time is a revealer. I'm a big believer in letting time do the telling.

The first Thanksgiving after our separation, I invited my son and ex-husband as well as other people that I wanted to be with us for Thanksgiving. I invited my ex for the kids. I left my daughter at home while I went to pick up some of my guests, and he arrived while I was gone. He was very upset that I made him wait and invited other people who were not on his chosen list. It was not acceptable to him. Even in this situation, he thought he had a right to control everything. I guess he did not get it. He took my son and daughter to McDonald's. He dropped her off after, and then left again. I didn't even get to see my son. After my guests left, I hid in bed the rest of the day. It was the first Thanksgiving I didn't spend with my son. I cried for two days, then prayed for patience.

Soon my son came to live with me. Things didn't get better right away, but I knew I wasn't the only one suffering. We all had a lot of pain and scars, physical and emotional. I knew I needed to be patient. My son was a teenager – and like any teen, had lots of things to figure out.

· · ·

Money

When we separated, my ex-husband took every penny we had with him. He left me in deep financial problems. We were in a lot of debt, and I was the only one left with the responsibility. I did not have any money so I wasn't able to hire a lawyer for the divorce. I did a "do-it-yourself" divorce. I did not have time for healing. I put aside my suffering. I told my pain that I would get back to it when I was ready to deal with it, and I went back to work to care for my family.

I wanted so much to protect my children so I worked very hard to give them a stable home. I didn't want them to see me being sad or depressed, but financially things were not going well. I wasn't able to pay all the debts I was left with. My house was about to go into foreclosure, but I was more concerned about my kids' reactions than losing the house. I wanted to tell my children and not have it be a surprise. I told my son that we might lose the house and not have a place to live for a while. He said, "As long as we are together, I don't care about the car, the house, or anything else. The most important thing is that we are together." I was so grateful for that response! Next, I went to my daughter and she said the same thing. Their support gave me courage to do more to save our home. Even though my house did not go into foreclosure, I had to struggle with many things. But I am so thankful for my children and their support and encouragement.

I am sad that my kids had to go through all of that. I did not want them to have this life experience at all. I had worked hard for them to grow up in a peaceful home where there was a mom and dad, but I was not successful in that. This nearly broke my heart.

Now things are a little different. With God's help, I have turned things around from a difficult situation in just little more than a year. Even though we still go through hard times, we always recover if we are patient. I've learned that nothing is more important that your loved ones. I used to collect antique tea sets and these were my prize possessions. But one day I realized that all those pretty dishes meant nothing anymore. We started using them for everyday. I have learned that I can detach myself from anything. But there is nothing more important than my family and God.

• • •

Depression and Domestic Abuse Effects on Women

Domestic violence is overwhelming. As victims of this senseless tragedy, our lives are routinely jeopardized, and our bodies and spirits battered and broken. We are often robbed of the money we work hard to earn. We lose family and friends, are socially isolated, withdrawn from all support, and made to feel powerless, stupid and worthless.

We put up with it because we think it is in the best interest of our children to have a home, which we fear, often accurately, we cannot provide on our own. We put up with it because we get so worn down that we have no energy to fight. We put up with it because to leave would mean to admit, to ourselves and others, the shame of how we have "allowed ourselves" to be treated. It would mean giving up any semblance of a normal, healthy family, which is our deepest desire. We fear that leaving would mean further abandonment, from church, family, friends, and community. We fear poverty. We fear what our abuser will do if we leave. And, most of all, we have no place to go.

This is true, generally, but is especially true for refugee women. We live in close communities where social taboos are strong. Divorce is not an acceptable option, no matter how severe the abuse is. Refugee women know they and their children need the support and approval of their community.

Children are also horribly beaten, though mothers more often step in and "take it" to protect their child. Then the children witness the battering and feel guilty that their mother suffers for them. They feel powerless because they can't help her. Sometimes they believe the battering is their fault, though they don't know what they did to cause it.

The tragic reality is that anytime a mother is abused the child is also affected, in both overt and subtle ways. They experience a steady diet of extreme confusion, stress, shame and fear. Children from abusive homes very often develop significant behavioral and emotional problems, including psychosomatic disorders, anxiety, fears, sleep disruption, crying and learning problems in school. The home ideal of love, care and protection is replaced by violence, fear and instability. Domestic abuse is a crime; we need to treat it as such!

• • •

Processing

Despite remarkably strong coping skills and the support of the many others who have already resettled in this country, many refugees continue to suffer from the effects of violence and war that we experienced in our home country before we fled along with the discomfort of readjusting to a new country.

The long-term effects of war trauma can be physical and/or psychological. A few years ago there were stories about a young woman who killed her six children, another woman who killed her four children by throwing them in the Mississippi River, and another who killed her husband. Each of these stories involved refugee families.

Those are just a few women who reacted violently, but there are many more that are not a threat to society or to their families but suffer silently. Their suffering can have a big effect on their jobs and family life. Many who were forced from their homes by violence experienced more suffering in refugee camp and have felt many effects on their lives. Those of us who have recovered from an emotional trauma need to reach out to help and support others.

Over the years, many women have shared their stories with me. Though I do not have permission to share their stories here, it is inspiring to realize the huge strength present in each human spirit. I was amazed to hear the similarities of hardship and silent suffering shared by so many women. It is good to share our stories. It is the best way to help others. If you are able and have the strength to share your story, I believe it will transform someone's life.

I have learned that not everyone has the strength to do this. The memories and pain are often still too fresh in their mind. But I heard an old story in Ethiopia. A man was walking barefoot on sand one hot day. He complained to God, "Why don't you give me shoes?" A few minutes later he saw a smiling man with only one leg, hobbling with a stick. The man without shoes came to his senses and told God, "It's okay for me to not have shoes. Thank you for my two legs."

I came to know many women, from many walks of life, who reminded me of that little story. I began to think my problems were not so big after all. Those women did not stop surviving. They did not focus on their circumstances, but on their strengths, and they drew encouragement and inspiration from one another. I learned that once we identify our barriers, there are always people out there who are willing to help. We may not all have a husband, family, or friend who will understand and support us in our challenges, but we can learn to de-emphasize our problems and reach out all the more. It is the best thing we can ever do for ourselves.

• • •

Depression

Although not all refugee women suffer from it, depression is a common experience among this group. Even though there are many reasons for it, the main thing is to recognize and deal with it and start enjoying life. The first step in finding relief is to accept yourself as you are and to acknowledge that you are depressed. I remember a long time ago someone told me that Christians do not suffer from depression, and I felt ashamed that I was dealing with depression. I thought there was something wrong with me because I was depressed and a Christian, but now I know that the Bible talks about depression many times, and it is not a sign of sin or weakness at all. Both the prophet Elijah and King David experienced depression. (1 Kings 19:1-18; 1 Samuel 30:3-6)

My depression was mostly because of the domestic abuse, both directly and indirectly. People sometimes told me they were afraid to be my friend and afraid to ask questions because they could see how it was affecting me, physically and emotionally, but they were afraid to interfere. They were afraid of my husband, but also, they felt powerless to help me. At the time I didn't realize how my depression was affecting me, or those around me.

I didn't value myself when I was depressed. I knew I had a problem and had to do something about it, but I felt powerless. I didn't know who to go to for help. Now people ask me why I didn't leave. There are lots of reasons, but mostly, I had no place to go. I had no friends or relatives to go to. I tried shelters a couple of times, but that kind of day-to-day situation didn't work. I wanted to go somewhere for a month at a time, at least. I thought I was trapped, and became resigned that this was how it was going to be for the rest of my life. I just had to accept that.

Now I understand that people who manipulate you have a way of making you feel like you are nothing, that you are not capable of doing anything. From hearing and feeling that so many times, my mind automatically believed I was powerless and worthless. Even though I was walking and breathing, I wasn't really living. Each day was a chore, a dull performance. I felt no joy or lightness but just existed in a heavy fog of routine. Go to work, come home, cook, clean... It was the same thing everyday. I was only half alive.

I allowed anything to happen to me for the sake of peace for my kids. It was too much to fight. Plus, I didn't feel that I had any rights or deserved anything better anyway. My real self slipped way down deep into me for protection. I think my superficial blankness gave my husband the idea that I was stupid or deserved punishment. But I let anything go as long as there was eventual peace. I was completely passive. In the back of my mind, though, I knew I wasn't happy at all. I knew that wasn't the life I wanted to live. I knew no living being should be treated that way.

• • •

Finding Solace

One time I went out of state to visit a friend for a couple of days with my two kids. There I met a woman from Ethiopia, educated in the U.S. A family physician, she also had the same faith as me. Even though this was the first time I met her, we connected, and I was able to be open and share everything that was going on in my life. She was the first person from my native country who I openly talked to about my problems. Knowing she was a doctor who knew how to deal with depression made it easier. Also, because she was a woman from my country and because she shared my faith I had confidence that she would be able to help me with my problems.

She answered my questions not only from a medical point of view, but from Christian, female, and cultural points of view as well. Those were the parts I was struggling with. I wanted to make sure that even if I separated, got out of my depression and marriage, I would be culturally appropriate and whole from both my Christian faith, and medical points of view. All these aspects were very important to me. I felt that God provided this woman at the right time to answer all my questions.

I continued communicating with her after those days as well. She confirmed to me that the decision I was going to make was going to be the right decision from all the points of view that I was concerned with. Based on that advice, and having someone available to talk to who could understand where I was coming from made a big impact in my life.

One thing that always amazed me was that at my workplace women would seek me out and talk to me about their problems. They said they could trust me, and I would help them solve their problems, even though I was secretly struggling with the same issues in my own life. Some of the women were single women, recently divorced. As they shared their problems, I wanted to tell them, but they looked at me as some kind of role model. Inside my heart, I wished I wore their shoes. I wished I had the courage they had.

These women took chances culturally, with their relatives, with approval from their children, but through it all, they encouraged themselves and had the courage to get out of abusive marriages. Yet they would still come to me; they admired what I did and wanted advice from me. I wanted to say to them, "I would give it all up to just have the courage you have." All I wanted to do was get out of my terrifying marriage, but could not yet figure out the way.

• • •

After the Flames

When I finally did have that courage and got out of my marriage, the first thing I wanted to do was work with those women and children. I saw so much need for this. I started an organization that could help them in any way I could. I started with very basic things, like taking them grocery shopping, or to hospitals and other places they needed to go. I helped them with their everyday needs because most of them did not have a car. Some had many small children. Imagine, winter in Minnesota, carrying groceries and kids at the same time.

Eventually, I wanted to know more than what I could learn in my circle. I wanted to know how refugee and new immigrant women were dealing with life in this country. I wanted to know what they were struggling with and what they were doing to make their lives better. I interviewed women from many different international communities – Eastern European, Asian, African, Latino. I was so surprised and impressed by what I learned.

· · ·

Refugee Women's Struggles With Finding Help

    Refugee women struggle with many issues. Most come from Asian, African, or Latino cultures where communities are very tight-knit. Women bond and help one another back in their home country. Their lives are not separate from one another. The whole village raises their families together. Working together, women can almost always find a way to solve the problems in their communities, including domestic violence and depression. What I have learned from talking to many women is that with so many women scattered and lost from these communities, the men are not being held accountable. The fabric of the community is so torn here that there are not many elders for them to be accountable to.

    Also, I think the society we live in is so much about independence that it allows some of our men or women not to be accountable to their community. The majority of them are not doing anything about it because of cultural issues and faith. Most of them also don't know where to go or what to do about their pain. Even though we live in the U.S., these women are still afraid to open up about their struggles. I have worked as an interpreter for women going to the doctor. Many times they won't say anything to the health care provider because of fear, but they will tell me about the abuse while we are in the waiting area. Every immigrant community sticks closely together and is closed, and those issues are very sensitive in these communities. You cannot go outside the community, or even inside the community, and talk about your issues with domestic violence. You cannot say that you are abused or depressed. This is a huge problem, thus people do not know how to seek help.

Even in America, well-educated women from other cultures have been dropped from their social circles and support when they "come out" about it. One woman had really been struggling with an abusive marriage. She had been abused physically. She had so many bruises all over, but she did not know how to explain them at work. She had run out of excuses for her bruises. When she finally divorced, her mother, entire family and friends deserted her. They told her that no one would marry her with two children. They were concerned about the family's reputation, not hers or her children's well-being. There is one single reason why the community or families do not work to change this: They deny the problem instead of supporting the victims. Women don't know how to get help or access information, even if they are educated. They have to make a choice between dealing with their problem and being deserted by their family and community members, or swimming in the soup of bruises and external approval.

In the Hmong community, there is no external way to receive support because a wife's job is to serve her husband. Her immediate point of contact is her husband's family, so there is no one to talk to in her immediate circle. This problem is not just with ordinary women. Professional women also struggle with it, even when they have an education and know how to access resources. It is still a decision of being cut off by their family and community. It is a big issue in our community and it is one bridge we are not able to cross yet.

Generally, depression is seen as a sign of weakness. Since a wife's primary responsibility is to her husband and family, her own depression is considered a selfish problem, and she is left to deal with it alone. We do not understand depression from a medical standpoint as a problem that needs to be solved. There is a solution for it, but when a person is depressed we view them as deficient or tainted in some way. We subtly believe they chose to be depressed instead of seeking the source of the problem.

Some women go to the doctor and are examined, but do not tell their doctors they are depressed. One woman said to me she just waited and hoped that the doctor would say the word "depression" so she could respond to it, but she wouldn't offer up the information. The doctor didn't want to put the words in her mouth, but all she wanted was to be diagnosed with depression. This is a large problem in our refugee community.

The other problem is that in our community when people have marriage problems, they don't believe in counseling. They don't want anyone to know that they have a marriage problem nor do they like to admit it to themselves. People just think the problems will solve themselves. Of course, most of the time they don't. Even though they value their marriage, people in these international communities don't seek marriage counseling or any other sort of outside help.

Because there seems to be no way to improve things, women often experience high levels of stress and depression. Every day, they get their kids to school, go to work, come home from work, cook, clean up, and put the kids to bed before they collapse themselves. There is no personal time for woman. Most of the time men don't feel stress because when they come home from work, they just go out with their friends. They rarely recognize that their wives are stressed out and that they could help by taking care of the children for the night, for example. They see that no matter what their wife is dealing with, it is her responsibility. One woman said that she doesn't think holidays are fun anymore. Her job from morning to night is to cook and prepare the festivity with no help. Then the guests come and eat, drink and leave, and the husband also leaves or relaxes so she is stuck with all the work afterward too.

When you experience these things every day, and cannot take it anymore, you finally may not care if your family or community throws you out of the circle. When you get out of the situation, you are judged as if you were a criminal. Sometimes, though, if that is what it takes you just have to do it.

• • •

Venturing Out

We now live in a country where there are a lot of options and resources; we don't need to think about hurting ourselves or others. When a person puts their mind to it, there is nothing they cannot do. I am a living testimony to that. Things were not easy for me when I first separated from my husband. I was left with a lot of financial and emotional responsibility. I struggled with the debts from the marriage – credit cards, mortgages, car loans – and the everyday expenses of life. It was nerve-wracking when collectors called. Mostly, I didn't want to fail my kids.

Many people saw me as a monster, but I knew what I was doing and I knew it was the right decision for me. I let people know that it isn't easy and you have to pay a price for it, but those costs were worth it for me because I knew if I lived one more day in that marriage I wouldn't have made it. It was that bad for me. I'm alive because of my decision. My kids have a mother because of my decision.

Through it all, I said to myself that I had come this far and I could make it. It occurred to me that I had been the one doing everything in my marriage anyway. I worked two jobs and did everything at home, including maintenance. I realized that if I could do all that then, with all the fear and hitting, I could certainly do it on my own. I made up my mind to not just save myself, but also to do whatever I could to make a difference in others' lives as well.

My healing process began when I began working with others who went through my experience. Hearing their stories and helping them find solutions was a daily dose of medicine for my recovery and motivated me to do more in my community. We may struggle in many ways, and have been bitter or angry at so many things or people that have done us wrong, but I didn't want to focus my energy on the past. I was just able to think it through and say, "God, I have been through that and what can I do now to make my life better?" We are able because God has put into each one of us a wonderful energy that we can use to make our lives and others lives so much better.

• • •

Dreams and Plans

I used to have so many dreams and visions of what I wanted to do in life, but if I talked about them, I was always laughed at. Today my dreams are alive. The dreams I never thought I could touch again, those dreams are alive. I am able to dream new dreams too, and those are already coming alive. I am able to do what I want to do. I know that I am not doing them all right now, but all the things that I am dreaming, they will happen.

One of my dreams was to start a center especially for women to come and feel at home and make friends, laugh, do something as a group, and just relax and forget their problems. I also wanted a center for the kids, so they would not be left behind when their moms are working hard to earn a living. They would not be left home alone. They would have a place to go, hang out, do their homework, enjoy time with their friends and get a reward for the good work they were doing.

So I quit my jobs and started this business in my basement. Within a year I opened a center, and today I am able to help a lot of women and their children. I reached for help, and now I am so grateful to the many great individuals and organizations which helped to bring my dreams to life.

I've learned that we can turn any type of bitterness or bad experience into a challenge to make us better people. I may work two or three jobs to make ends meet, but I can do that. I believe that we should not be bitter and angry. We should focus our energy into positive action because that is the way to heal and help others. We may experience dark times and feel like our dreams are dead and buried, and we may look at our lives and see insurmountable problems. But those experiences and problems are often opportunities with a special purpose. I believe that God is shaping us and preparing us for what he wants us to do in life.

I have plenty of excuses for failure: I had no parents; my brothers were killed; I was raped and tortured and lived in a refugee camp; I was torn from my homeland and deposited in a foreign country; I have endured dramatic domestic abuse and have experienced chronic back pain. Instead of being bitter or sad about it, I am looking at it in a good way. I know that God has a purpose in my life and wants to make me a stronger person. The more things we go through in life, the deeper and stronger we can become. It is our choice how we see things.

My experiences have opened my heart so I can understand what others are going through. Growing up with no parents has taught me how it feels to have nobody there for me. If I run into a person who is alone in life I can understand and be compassionate toward this person. Our experiences can shape us into bitter people or better people. We can choose. Hard experiences can also help us become good problem solvers. We have been there, we know how it feels to have that problem, and we can help find a solution for it. No one will understand a problem as well as a person who has gone through it.

• • •

Happy On My Own

My struggles have helped me realize my priorities. Shortly after I left my marriage, a friend asked me if I was dating anyone. It hadn't even crossed my mind. I was just beginning to heal! When we go through such big changes we need to take time to learn and recover from our experiences. We need to evaluate what went wrong, what we can improve on, and how to prepare for the future.

I had children, and I knew a relationship would affect them. Looking at my situation and my life, I realized it wasn't right for me then. I wanted to focus on creating a stable home for my kids. My first priority was that they would have a mother whenever and for whatever reason they needed her. I also wanted to create financial independence for myself. I didn't want to bring anyone into my financial mess. Later on, even if the relationship wasn't the best, I didn't want to feel obligated to stay in it because they might have helped me financially. And I certainly didn't want to be financially dependent on another person. For now I am happy to focus on my kids, have them finish school, and be available whenever they need me. I will not divide my time between dates and my children's lives. It is important to me to give full attention to my children.

Sometimes, as women, we think that bringing a man into our children's lives will be a good thing for them. Maybe that's right. But we don't have to mix that with finding a new partner. I think there are many ways to have a male influence for children. We need to be strong and clear for ourselves before we get involved with someone else. Emotionally and physically there are so many adjustments to make. Simply changing the man in our life will not solve any problems. It is good to take time to see what our own interests and dreams are. There are so many things that we are finally able to do. Explore these things. See how it feels to be single and whole.

· · ·

Overcoming Challenges

I think the past four years have been the most challenging in my life. But also the best because I've been able to use strengths I didn't know I had. I have solved problems and coped in ways I never could have imagined. And I have a solid foundation in my faith now. I told my friends that I had heard about God for so many years. Now I know Him.

Some of the challenges I have met? Right after my depression I started my own business. I run a center for women and children with all expenses paid by me and with no capital or experience. I have dealt with many of the challenges common to small business owners, especially financial, including covering the expense to get the business up and running. Working long days with no break was normal. But I learned what it takes to be a businesswoman in this culture.

One of the things I did in my business was to help new immigrant women get work experience. I found cleaning contracts and hired women who had no work experience at all. Training was a challenge because many had never used a vacuum cleaner or even a broom before. It took a lot of patience, kindness, creativity and dedication to teach adult women these skills without offending or embarrassing them. Then, after a woman was trained and doing good work, I would ask her to leave and find a better job, using me as a reference. This was a good idea for them, but I always lost my best workers. And I learned the hard way that some people just want the job for money but have no commitment to do the job well. So a lot of the responsibility fell on me.

After my divorce, the courts granted me the house, which came with a mountain of debt and responsibility. I did not know how I was going to pay all the bills, even though I had my own business. The first year was the most difficult because most of the people I did business with were late in their payments to me. I sent out invoices on time, but received the payments late. I got behind on some of my bills and almost lost my house. The phone calls from collectors almost drove me crazy. And I did not have anyone to share my burden. But with a lot of work, some time, and God's help this also passed.

If we make improving our lives our number one priority, a new life, is waiting for us. Just as I go through my house once in awhile to get rid of things I do not need anymore, I go through my days to see what I don't need to think, feel and do anymore. These things all take my energy – a little here, a little there. What is important to me is to focus my energy on what matters most. Focusing on my family and putting my energy toward that is the most important thing for me. I cannot waste my energy. I cannot settle for constant worrying.

If you are struggling through a tough time, it can be an opportunity for you to discover new and more effective ways of dealing with things. Continue learning. Focus your energy on what is most important to you. Do not waste your energy. Your energy is your life.

I met a woman who shared her story proudly. She said "I never left my house before I met you. I have four children, and I did not know how to find a job or what to do about my children's day care. But I got help and met other women who have been able to overcome their difficulties. Now my limit is the sky." Most of the time we just have to have the courage and willingness to go as far as life can take us. If you truly believe in yourself and are clear about what is most important to you, you will quickly discover what you need to do and will have enough energy to do it.

• • •

Advice

It has been worth it to look back and learn from my experiences. My advice to any woman is simply that life is too short, so do not spend it all on worry, revenge or holding grudges.

Being in a totally new place in life is overwhelming. This does not only include physical location, but also major changes in life, such as a marriage, a new family member or a death in the family. Make a goal to meet a new person each day or to do something new every day. Do not think that no one will care. If you give enough time to people and blend with them, you will find out that all humans have some things in common.

If you see things that need to be changed or fixed, make a habit of learning and doing it yourself instead of waiting for someone else to do it. Think of yourself as part of a large society. Your effort and input can make a difference.

Share your experiences and be eager to learn from others as well. An old proverb from my country says, "God gave me good looks, I'll learn the rest from my neighbor." Be a responsible person and keep your word. I know that many of our cultures taught us to never say no. But in our new culture it is best to say no when you are not able to do something. Otherwise we will be considered unreliable and things won't go very well for you. So if you say you are going to be at a certain place at a certain time, you should be there. If you say you are going to do something, then you should do it. This way people can rely on you.

Life is like a farm. Whatever you sow, you will reap. Focus more on giving than on getting. When you do things, do more than your share. That is a good work ethic. Be accountable to yourself and to others. Don't be difficult to live or work with. Avoid thinking everyone else is wrong.

Making a friend requires a lot of give and take. Always find a middle ground. Make an effort to be a good friend. Whatever we give will come back to us, multiplied.

Sometimes, when you try really hard, your reward may not pay back. You may not be satisfied. Again, you must be patient and should not expect an immediate reward. Perhaps your reward will happen for your offspring or a future generation. But be nice through this and don't be mean. Even if a reward never transpires, it is always worth it to be nice. Just do the next thing by putting one foot in front of the other. The thing you are capable of doing is exactly the right thing to do. We need to learn that everything takes time and we can only do one thing at a time, so take baby steps.

One thing I have learned is that when we face uncertainty we must be diligent and pursue excellence while we wait for things to work in our favor. I have learned that when I have given all I can and there is nothing more I can do, there is peace in just surrendering it all to God's will. Something good always comes of this, though it isn't always what I thought I wanted. I have realized success is not just money or possessions. It can be health, children, a good job or friendships. All these things are blessings. Success is not what you have; it is what you can do and how you can think. Think positively and do all you can do.

Often when I look at a big problem in my life, I think there is no way out of this – I will never make it this time. But then I tell myself that I need to find a positive attitude. I look for my blessings and what God has done for me in the past. I look at the hardship and ask for it to make me stronger. Then I just roll up my sleeves and do what needs to be done. We can take any day and turn it to our advantage, rise to accept the opportunities in our challenges, and see that disadvantage and discouragement are just stones on our larger path.

We refugees can feel overwhelmed. It can feel like we don't have what we need to meet the needs of those who depend on us, and we don't see how to do all that needs to be done. It seems like there are endless tasks! It is true that most of us do not have experience in this modern lifestyle, which is all about self-sufficiency. Most of us come from a culture and tradition that believes it takes a village to raise a family. But here, in our adopted culture, independence is a basic value and requirement.

How do we balance this? It's important to see the difference between being independent and being separate. Independence is about the relationship between personal responsibility and freedom. It means to be free from outside control, not depending on another's authority or resources, capable of thinking or acting for oneself. This doesn't mean we have to do everything by ourselves, not offering or asking for help. We don't have to be separate from other people.

We must each start where we are, know where we want to go and work hard to get there. It is up to us to design our own life and chart our path through it. We must be flexible and keep a broad perspective.

Sometimes, when things are difficult for me here, I take a step back to review why I came to this country in the first place. I'm here because of my will to survive the war and terror in my home country and because I was fortunate. I think the family members I have lost along the way would want me to make a better life for my children and myself. Why are you here? Now that you are, what do you want, and what are you going to do about it?

It's important to make some quiet alone time for yourself. This has been so important in helping me put things in perspective. It gives me the time I need to put my thoughts and prayers in order. Set a regular silent time for you alone to think through things and relax. If you like walking, go for a walk by yourself. If you enjoy bubble baths, do that. Sometimes it is good to write down your thoughts. Make sure you won't be interrupted. Turn off the phone. Even if it's just for five minutes, make it your own time. If none of this is the way you relax then do whatever relaxes you. It's also helpful to spend some time with someone you trust, just doing whatever you feel like doing.

I also suggest a daily devotion time. It will help you release what you've been holding in your heart and mind. I have my devotion time late at night because that is the best time for me to release what went on during the day. Also, I'm not a morning person. Use what time works best for you.

• • •

Refugee Stories

The following three stories are based on interviews with individuals and community leaders. Their candidness, advice and suggestions help us understand how much we have in common. We can learn a lot from them and use it to help ourselves and other refugees.

Afghani Woman's Story

The problems started when the Russians came to my country and my family didn't want the communists to take over Afghanistan. Our family, especially my dad's side of the family, was the community leader. The majority of people in our village were against the takeover. We knew that since my father was the person who made decisions in the village, we would be the first targets for the Russians. At night, about one or two in the morning I think it was, four years into my marriage, they came. Russians knocked on my father's door saying they didn't have food or other things and since my dad was the village leader, would he help the newcomers? Only my grandfather and my uncle – the one who was in high school – were at home. So the Russians took out these two and shot them just two blocks down the street. They then stole everything, even the couch pillows. That's how far they went.

My mother was two blocks down from where they were all living. Some kids came and told her that her father and her brother had been shot. She doesn't remember what happened after that.

After they killed my mother's father and my uncle, they came looking for my father. They broke in through the door, so he had to climb the wall between homes to escape. He got to Pakistan. After my father moved, he thought it would be better for my mother to move to Pakistan too.

All this happened in 1980, one year after the Russians arrived. Then a year after that, they came looking for my other uncle, who was a doctor in the military. He had seven daughters and two sons. Only five of his children remember him. I think he is in prison.

Five years later, my mother's uncle was targeted. He didn't have a lot of money. He was out working in his field and someone just came and shot him. They killed him. They really had anger towards my mother's side of the family because my grandfather and oldest uncle had been the main leaders in the village.

They killed the brother of mom's sister's daughter-in-law. As a result she had a miscarriage. After that she wasn't able to have kids. God knows how many people were killed. There was a night when the Russians killed twenty-five people and threw the bodies like they were animals. There was another lady in the village whose husband was killed. After she saw her husband's body, she committed suicide.

People didn't go in the daytime to get the bodies. They used to go at night and walk with candles and lanterns because in the daytime the helicopters would fly over. Whatever they had to do, they did at night. The Russians would bombard people. Families used to bury people at night. They wouldn't know what things looked like until morning.

I could sit here and tell the whole world the stories but not everyone can feel the stories. How can someone just come to your house and bomb and kill everyone?

There is a saying that the only person who feels the burning is the one in the fire. Others may see the fire and know it's hot, but only the one burning feels it. Refugees understand because we have felt the fire burning our own flesh. We have experienced war and everything that goes with it.

We have been anxious and nervous for so long. We have never had time to grieve for our lost husbands, siblings, parents, children, friends. We don't forget how we survived the grueling days when we fled our country or what we endured in the refugee camps, often as young mothers, with many children and no husband or resources.

Even after resettlement we worked long hours for low pay in a constant dash to jump the next moment's hurdle. Though guns are no longer aimed at our heads, the pressure to survive has never let up. There has been no time when we could finally say, "Let me rest and grieve, let me clear my mind."

Hmong Women

One of the reasons I decided to write this book was because of the Hmong women I've met. Remember the Hmong woman who killed her six children? A typical American cannot begin to understand why she did what she did. They think it's a horrible thing. But other refugees understand, because we know how it feels. We've usually been made to marry too young, have had too many children, have too many responsibilities and not enough opportunities, and lose hope for a future we want to take part in. All the war, the refugee camps, the injustice, the loss, the struggle of resettlement – it's too much. We sink lower and lower into depression.

One way to react is the way that woman did – by using the only power she had left to end the suffering. It happens in every refugee community.

Refugees are usually not only responsible for their family here in the United States, but for their family remaining in their home country or in refugee camps somewhere else. We came from war zones where we've seen our parents and other loved ones be tortured and or killed. Usually, we too have suffered terrible violence and physical hardship. All these experiences get thrown in a pile, with rage and grief, for us to deal with later when we get the chance. But the challenges we face to just survive in this new country are huge and relentless. We need help, but don't know where to turn or how to ask.

I worked as a nurse in my country. Before I came to the United States, I knew I would need to learn English, but I thought my nursing education would carry over. I brought nothing with me from home but this. But when I arrived, I learned that not even my education and profession were useful here. I had to do everything over. For a woman with home responsibilities and children, that's really tough.

Many refugee women are illiterate when they come here. They

are not able to write their names or say the alphabet. It's a major issue. At home we had many responsibilities. We had to take care of our family, be a full-time housekeeper and wife, and have food on the table from six in the morning until six at night. Every day we had house chores, all kinds of tasks that we were assigned, especially by our husbands. These were the ways we gained respect in our home communities. But, when we came here, our work became invisible. Many more responsibilities were added to our existing burden.

As women, we have to be involved in the community to be able to survive here. We have to develop new survival skills besides what we already had, because everything is different. We need leadership and cohesiveness, all access to resources to help us handle the many new things that will otherwise make us crazy. Even in our own homes we need to carve out a different role and manage things differently than before. We have to change the way we work with our families.

Stress and depression have a huge impact on everyone, married and single, young and old. Many immigrants are able to take control and manage their stress and their situation. They just try to get around and to have patience. They re-educate themselves. But others, refugees and immigrants, lose their grip and give up. That's why we have so many things going on in our community. There is so much change that they have nothing more to cling to or build on. Almost all of us struggle financially, and most of our talk is of these matters.

Men's roles and responsibilities are also very different here. Back home there were elders to tell them what was right and wrong. But here, they are on their own. They have to make their own decisions. They don't have anyone to go to and consult to get a second opinion. So many men make mistakes and often lose their way. This causes a major change in the family structure. The women, the wives and children, must take up the slack. This adds even more stress and depression to women's lives.

Unfortunately, other people, including family members, do not recognize depression and stress. A person may keep going to people to ask for help or tell her family members that she's upset or she's depressed or that she will commit suicide. But people never take her seriously. People say, "Don't kill yourself—you have to think about your children. Just be patient and one day things will get better." That is not a helpful answer.

I've seen a lot of women commit suicide because nobody said, "You have a problem, let me help you." The thing that makes me really sad is here in the United States there is a support system in place. It's possible for us to get help.

There are many resources available, but first a person must see that they need it. We must learn to see abuse as a crime, not a shame, and depression as a consequence, not a cause. We won't seek help if we don't realize we need it or are too ashamed to seek it.

American organizations are based on a belief that we already understand how to access the available resources. They assume that when we come from Africa or Asia we already know about American systems, but we don't. We are not here on business. We came here because of war. We came here because we were forced to and not because we chose to. Some of us came here from the worst of conditions, but we don't know what to expect when we get here. We have no idea what we are getting ourselves into or what we will face. Maybe it will be better; maybe it will be the same or worse. Will we survive? Will we get killed? Will people be nice or will they be mean? We don't know.

There are so many areas where we need to be educated. We often don't know the policies or rules in the United States regarding peoples' rights. We need to talk about these things, but don't know where to begin. We're talking about human rights. We're talking about child support. We're talking about women's rights. We're talking about so many things—rules and regulations that make sense to Americans, but which are foreign – unknown and nonsensical – to us. We learn these very gradually, and often at great cost. A refugee is always absorbing new information, even when they are too full to process it.

A Somali Woman's View

I spoke with a Somali community leader about life before and life after becoming a refugee and a resident of the United States.

Many Americans don't know that immigrant women and immigrant families usually had a good life before the war – before becoming refugees. Many are highly educated and had a very good life, but it was interrupted by war, a police situation, a religious situation. Then they were forced to leave their country as a refugee. First, they have the refugee camp, and then they come to the U.S. and are expected to fit into society like a typical American. But they have lost everything some don't act normal, and nobody is trying to find out why.

I'm from Somalia. I was educated and received a bachelor's degree in agricultural economy. In 1984, I started teaching at the university. Then, after six years, war broke out. Everything was destroyed. People were killing each other. It was a very tough life, especially for women.

We went to be refugees in Kenya. When the UN went to Somalia, I returned also. I worked with a women's organization helping those who had been raped. I also got a nice job working for UNICEF. I was working with a political office as an adviser and working with the reconciliation conference. At the end, when things were not going smoothly and the international community couldn't reconcile, they pulled out.

I left the country and came to the United States. When I came, I didn't speak English. My background was Somali and Italian and Arabic, so I started ESL (English as a Second Language) classes. After one year I was able to go to work, but had no other assistance. It was very difficult for me.

For the first four to five months I was here, I felt myself becoming mentally desolate. I began having nightmares remembering what happened in Somalia. I would dream and see people killed in front of me. Or I would remember the women who had been raped. This was always coming into my mind. When I was in Somalia I didn't have bad dreams because I was in the middle of the turmoil, but when I came here they began. If a spoon fell down on the ground or a door closed loudly, I would be startled. But, at that time, I didn't realize the connection. I didn't know the meaning of depression or stress. Soon after, when I was going to school, working, and helping my kids, I was so angry; I was shouting at everyone. Later I realized that it was the post trauma of the war. In working with Somali women you see that frequently.

Recently, I was working with a Somali woman, and she was shouting and saying whatever she wanted to me. She didn't realize that she was in the office. I could have called the authorities, but I didn't because I knew what she was feeling. If it had been another person, an American person, she wouldn't have accepted that behavior. This woman was really damaging my feelings by what she was saying. However, I was feeling really sorry for her; I saw that she was not okay, and understood where the anger was coming from.

The one thing we see every day at the workplace, at the market place, and in the public place is people's reaction to whatever they are remembering in the back of their mind. American society is not open to know yet, or at least is not educated enough about all these things. We need to help the community understand why we act the way we act.

Workplaces need to have a lot of workshops explaining our background, especially what we were before the war. They need to understand that I never thought that I would come here to live, because my country was like a paradise for me. I never thought that I would go outside of Somalia to live because I had everybody and everything there. And then we came here. It's a very different experience, and it needs a lot of education. We have to educate the community and explain our background and situation.

The decision to come here was not our choice really. We didn't say that we had to go to America to find a job and live there. I was living in Somalia. I had my husband, my neighbors, my cousins; everybody I needed was around me. And I was happy to be with them. I never dreamt of going to America because we had our own life. In Somalia, if you are in the workplace, you have your own house. If you are a farmer, you have your own farm; you cultivate and sell your production. And you don't think that others exist. Your world is the world. You don't even know America. I remember when I was working at the university, and we were doing research at farms. An Italian professor went with me to one of the farms. The farmer, when he saw the white man, told him to not come into his farm because he may damage it. He didn't know the existence of this person. It was too strange for him, so he didn't allow him to come to his farm.

We didn't come here to take American people's jobs. We came here for different reasons. I believe that if they have peace in Somalia again, most of the people will go back because they will be happy. Over here, the women are not happy. They are getting more stressed every day because the life they used to live and this life are so very different, and it's hard for them.

The other thing I would like to speak of as an East African is that, in our tradition, women have a very strong support system. We have our moms, our grandparents, our sisters, and our brothers' wives. We have a support system when we have a baby.

In Somalia, when people marry, their household doesn't start with two people. It starts with four to five people. It includes the wife's sister or cousin, or maybe the husband's sister or cousin. They all live together. At a minimum, it starts with four. Even if you are a professional woman working outside the home, you can hire a maid to take care of the house. But our husbands don't do any housework because we don't need them to. We have a support group and we all work together.

When a woman gets pregnant, and then has a child, her time is only for sleeping, feeding and resting – always resting for 40 days. The support group does the rest of the work. After 40 days, a sister, a mother, and a cousin will still help. Someone cooks, someone watches the other children, and someone cleans the house. We grew up with that life – having a home where there are a lot of people who will help you. Even now, if my sister has a baby, I will go to her house and stay for 2-3 days to help her. That was our way.

Now that we are in the United States, there's no help. The salary is not high enough to pay for what we need to live, so both men and women have to work. In our culture, even if the woman works, it's still she who is responsible at home. East African men are not educated to work at home; that's an insult for them. They don't think it's their job to do chores. The man and the woman can both come home from work at the same time, but only the wife has to go to the kitchen and cook. She has to prepare everything and put it on the table. He will not come until everything is ready for him. He does nothing. He thinks it's not his responsibility. This makes a lot of stress for the woman. And more work. If the woman complains and tells him that they need to work together, he says she doesn't value the family. Some women, however, really keep the value of the family and ask in a polite way. Maybe then their husbands will help. Some women try to create a support group of women who work and try to find out a way to involve their husbands more.

First, women have to come together, and realize our common problems. Then we can find a way to address our husbands in a way that they can help us, and be involved in the housework and taking care of the kids and doing errands. I think also that American women have been in the situation. There was a time when it was only the woman's responsibility at home. How did they survive it? How did they overcome the problem? We will get experienced people, including psychologists, to help us. First, though, we have to find a way to get a group of East African women who can do an analysis to find out a way. If we educate the men, then women's stress, and its related illnesses, can be eased.

Stress can lead to illness, but we've been taught to just be strong and ignore it and keep on living. We may need to go to the doctor, but don't want to be embarrassed, or consider it a sign of weakness. Let's use the example of breast cancer. Just like depression, African women also do not know about breast cancer. It is something that is very rare back home. When we came here it was difficult to tell them that they needed to get a mammogram. We also did a lot of education, as everything comes back to education. We have to educate the women. It has to be in many languages, including Somali and Oromo, in community newsletters and other publications. We have media and we have to show them how this problem affects them.

Stress also comes from lack of finances, time and activity. Usually, both parents work heavy labor jobs, and there is a lot of fatigue and tiredness. So they don't spend a lot of time doing activities with their kids. But they can get help from their neighbors. Most of the refugees and immigrant people live in apartment buildings. They are populated in one area. So, people who are willing to help them may be in their building. They can explain what is going on. When people talk, they can find a solution.

I was working with a group of Somali girls at a high school. Their mothers were allowing them to go out and do activities. I went to one girl's house and I asked her mother if she could hold a meeting. All the other mothers were sitting there and talking about how we can help our girls. If you start by going to one apartment and invite the other ladies, when they start talking and see the benefit of things, then they will go out. We did not have these kinds of activities back home. Women didn't have activities. When a woman finished her housework, she would go to the neighbors and visit or would go shopping. She had a life; she was free. But here, they are in their apartment. The only entertainment they have is the TV and the phone. If they are not coming out, we have to go to them.

I agree. I worked for Common Bond, a very large, non-profit, affordable housing group in Minnesota. They own a lot of apartment buildings. I worked in two high-rise buildings. My department was to help the families who live there become active in many programs. Most of the time, the kids attended, but not the parents. When you are around your kids all the time at home, that in itself is stressful. When you live in a small apartment and there isn't room for the children to run around, it can drive parents crazy. But we can make something out of our situation. To be active in a community sometimes takes that negative energy away from the apartment and into the community space, where it can dissipate. Then everybody can feel better.

Conclusion

"She who conceals her disease cannot expect to be cured."
- Ethiopian proverb

For Refugee Women: How to Recognize Signs of Trauma

If you are a refugee woman and have had harmful things done to you or loved ones during the war, you may now have problems with sleeping or eating, or with the way you feel. You may:
- Have bad dreams at night or have trouble sleeping

- Have headaches, stomach aches, diarrhea, or muscle pain
- Be losing or gaining weight
- Feel sad or angry or without hope
- Be forgetful or not able to pay attention
- Feel as if you cannot control your thoughts and memories
- Be very tired
- Feel sick quite often and the doctor cannot find what is wrong with you
- Feel that others do not understand how you feel
- Feel that you can't trust anyone
- Worry all the time about your family

These things do not mean you are going crazy or have a permanent mental illness. These are normal reactions to the terrible things that have happened. You did not deserve what happened to you and you do not deserve to continue to be in pain.

Every one has one or two of these problems sometimes. But if you have more than two or three of these problems, or have even one that gives you trouble and makes it hard to get through the day, tell someone so that you may receive help. In the United States, there is help for people who are having problems because bad things happened to them in the past. Here are just a few organizations you can contact to get started. The most important thing is to reach out and get help.

Center for Victims of Torture (1-877-265-8775) www.cvt.org
Department of Health* www.health.state.mn.us
International Institute for Refugees* www.iimn.org
Lutheran Social Services* www.lssmn.org

*Note: the phone numbers for these agencies vary by city, state, or region. Please contact the agency for your area.

Acknowledgements

This book could only come together with the help of many extraordinary people. To all of you who put aside your own busy life to help me make my dream come true, I offer my deepest, most heartfelt thanks.

That being said, there is a group of you that I must single out, because I'm quite sure you don't fully realize what a blessing you have been in my life.

- To my good friend, Suzanne Kochevar, and your dear family, thank you for your encouragement and support over the years.
- To Ann Rock, Marlene Kakaliouras and the Women of Stillwater, MN Presbyterian Church, I offer my gratitude for your prayers and support.
- To my good friends Jill Johnson, Mona Carloni, Chryell Walsh Bellville, Marcie Rendon, Carol Williams, Lynda Shaheen, Phillip Vu, Antoni Tang, Brooke Girma Dalu, Marina Kalinichev, Connie Dow, Evelynn Lenon: Each one of you entered my life at exactly the right time. I can't begin to measure your positive impact. All of your patience, insight, generosity, and commitment to my vision has made a significant impression in my life and in my work. A wholehearted thanks to you all!
- To my pastor, Randy Morrison, thank you for instilling in me the peace and purpose that only come through a personal relationship with Jesus Christ. Also, thank you for teaching me to live my life by design, and not merely from crisis to crisis.
- To Dr. Mensa Otabil, just for being in my pastor's life in time of need, thank you.
- To my business partner and sister, Frewoini Haile, thank you for standing with me. I love you!

- I would also like to honor those who have inspired me and mentored me throughout my involvement in the community: Barbara Jeanetta, Joe Selvaggio, Paul Fate, and Hussein Samatr. I am so blessed to know you.
- To my children, I offer my endless gratitude and love for your patience and support. I thank God for trusting me to bring you into the world.
- Menase, I wish I could say life is not accompanied by pain and suffering, but we both know that's not true. Be strong and know that
- God is always with you. Make time to reflect on the many lessons life will offer you, and keep an open mind. More than anything, let the Word of God be the center of your life. I am so very proud of you!
- Asnat, thank you for your loving constancy. You share my joy when I'm up and my tears when I'm down. I'm deeply fortunate to be your mother. You are my best friend. You are the best daughter a mother could ask for. I love you!
- I would especially like to thank my amazing editors Sandra Turner and Janice Bady. To my chief editor, Sandra, your time, effort, dedication, and beautiful work are greatly appreciated! I am so grateful that you are in my life! I hope we will do many, many more books together!
- Dr. Jennifer A. Skuza, thank you for writing my foreward, being my friend, and for working with me on so many projects.
- And finally, it's impossible to thank here all the wonderful and generous people who have contributed to and enriched my life in less specific or obvious ways. Even so, my heart is filled with gratitude. It takes a village to write a book!

• • •

Update January 2014
My Return to Ethiopia

Arriving at the place where I started after all these years gave me loads of mixed feelings. Many years ago God had spoken to my heart saying, "I have a future and a plan for your life. My plan is to prosper you, not to harm you." It wasn't easy to imagine this when all I could see was my present condition and circumstance. But today, almost three decades later, I can say yes - He did have a plan and a purpose for my life. This is also true for the refugees still in these camps.

This is what I'm bringing to a refugee camp in northern Ethiopia. I come to tell them that even though their circumstances don't indicate it, God has a plan and a purpose for their lives - He does have a plan. I know it is easy for those here, especially the women, to think of themselves as a mistake - they have been told this, many times. When they look at the present circumstance they are in, a good life does seem hopeless. But God never made a mistake by creating mankind.

I am so grateful to God for giving me this opportunity to come back to the refugee camps. I am excited about the opportunity to teach them what I have learned and to show them the possibilities awaiting them. I am also learning new things for myself; the camps are completely different. When I was a refugee, we were numbered in the low thousands. In today's camps the refugees are counted in the hundreds of thousands and the problems they are facing are completely different than what I endured. Food shortages and poor water supply remain a common problem, but added to that, today's refugees are falling victim to human trafficking and the illicit organ trade as well as other problems such as mental illness.

These are just a few of the problems I am learning of but I have also witnessed uplifting and encouraging stories. I have talked to a 15-year-old boy who has such a love for boxing that even though it's impossible he made a way to practice his sport. He crafted a punching bag out of a water container and old clothing. His training weight is a stone he lifts everyday to build his body. He knows someday he will be out of this camp so he's working towards his goal that is more than a refugee's story. That was inspiring. I also met a 32-year-old woman who lost her mother and father, and as the oldest child, she felt responsible for her younger siblings so she opened a restaurant. She worked long hours to do everything necessary so her younger brother could attend school. These are but a few of the incredibly awesome and inspiring stores I have witnessed.

For me, seeing this many refugees is not an easy thing. There is a lot of work that needs to be done here. In March of 2014, *Woman At The Well* (an organization I founded) just broke ground on a multi-purpose education building at a refugee camp here in northern Ethiopia. This multi-purpose building will be used to teach language and life skills to help refugees adapt when they are placed in their new home. The building will also be used for spiritual awareness and faith based teaching. Another use is to provide education to the refugees about the threats and abuses associated with the growing problem of human trafficking. I see a great need for a clinic, not only for physical health, but mental health as well. Also a library and playground to provide different activities for the children and teenagers - the needs here seem endless.

I know the school is just the beginning and here at *Woman At The Well*, my dream and our mission is to create an avenue to address these issues. It is my goal to come back every year to expand this endeavor and continue the mission.

Shegitu Kebede

Special Acknowledgements
— *For invaluable service and support* —

- **Lake Minnetonka Excelsior Rotary Club**
- **International Institute of Minnesota**

I want to extend a heartfelt thanks to all my supporters for your contributions to this project, may God bless you immeasurably.

If you would like to partner with us financially or with other needed support please contact me via:

http://shegitukebede.wordpress.com
shegitu.kebede@wordpress.com
shegitukebede@gmail.com
612-290-8360